Excel

ADVANCED SKILLS

ENGLISH

YEAR 6

AGES 11–12

ADVANCED ENGLISH

Get the Results You Want!

PASCAL PRESS

Tanya Dalgleish

Contents

Introduction

The aim of the ***Excel*** **Advanced Skills: Advanced English** series is to build on and extend students' skills in English. Each book in the series supports the requirements of the Australian Curriculum English at each year level.

The series consists of six books, one for each year level, from Year 1 to Year 6. The series is supported by other books in the ***Excel*** **Advanced Skills English** range.

Structure of the book

Each book in the series contains:

- thirty carefully graded, three-page units of teaching and learning activities.
  - Unit A includes a sample informative, imaginative or persuasive text and deals with **Reading and comprehension skills**.
  - Unit B deals with the Conventions of language: **Spelling**, **Vocabulary**, **Grammar** and **Punctuation**.
  - Unit C deals with **Texts in context**. It provides for a deeper analysis and evaluation of the language choices authors make and the ways that readers make meaning from texts.
- four NAPLAN-style tests.
- answers for all questions.

How to use this book

- Students should complete one unit per week. A suggested plan would be to complete the week's Unit A and B page on one day and the Unit C page on another day of the same week.
- After successfully completing a set of units (e.g. 1–7, 8–15, 16–23, 24–30), students should undertake the corresponding NAPLAN-style test.

How to use this book with the *Excel* Advanced Skills: Advanced Mathematics series

For a complete **weekly English and Mathematics program**, use this book in conjunction with the ***Excel*** **Advanced Skills Advanced Mathematics Year 6** book. This way a student will have work set for four days a week: two days for English and two days for Mathematics.

Excel
ADVANCED SKILLS
MATHS
YEAR 6
AGES 11–12
ADVANCED MATHEMATICS
Get the Results You Want!
Allyn Jones

How to assess students' progress

- Templates are included in each book of the series that outline the knowledge and skills targeted by the questions in that book. (Please see page 6.)
- The questions move through the subtopics of English in exactly the same order in each book but as there are more questions and more complex material included in later years of the Year 1 to Year 6 continuum, the question numbers vary across the books.
- The results of the work undertaken in Units A and B can be recorded on the marking grid. See ways to use the marking grid on page 4.

Excel Advanced Skills titles

If students are having difficulty in any area, further support is available in other ***Excel*** workbooks. Please see the comprehensive list on page 5.

The *Excel* step-by-step improvement plan

Step 1

Read the introduction on page 3.

Step 2

Read the text below, along with the further explanation about the question templates and marking grids, on pages 6 and 7.

Question templates

These outline the knowledge and skills targeted by the questions in the book. Remember that the questions move through the subtopics of English in exactly the same order.

Marking grids

The results of the work undertaken in Units A and B can be recorded on the marking grid. This is an easy-to-use diagnostic tool that indicates each student's strengths and weaknesses in relation to specific areas of English.

These results can be used to gather extra information about each student's progress and revision needs. For example, see the Sample marking grid in the right-hand column:

- When marking answers on the grid, simply mark incorrect answers with 'X' in the appropriate box. This will result in a graphical representation of areas needing further work. An example for the first five units is shown above. If a question has several parts, it should be counted wrong if one or more mistakes are made.
- Remember that you can identify exactly what type of questions a student is having difficulty with in a topic. For example, in the grid above the student is having difficulty with Reading and comprehension evaluative questions.
- There is no marking grid for Unit C.

Marking grid

Reading and comprehension	Literal	Literal	Inferring	Inferring	Evaluative	Evaluative
Question	**1**	**2**	**3**	**4**	**5**	**6**
Unit 1						
Unit 2						X
Unit 3						
Unit 4						X
Unit 5						X
Unit 6						
Unit 7						
Unit 8						
Unit 9						
Unit 10						

This grid indicates that the student needs extra help and practice in evaluative questions.

Step 3

Refer to page 5: *Excel* books to help you *get the results you want*!

- Under each topic there is a list of books in our range to help students. Each ***Excel*** book has a comprehensive contents page that will help you find the appropriate pages in the book to target the specific topic you want in each subject area.

Excel books to help you *get the results you want!*

Reading and comprehension

Excel **Advanced Skills**

9781741254808

Excel **NAPLAN*-style Tests**

9781741254181

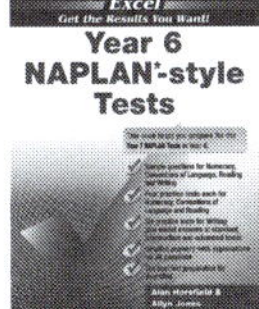

9781741253887

Spelling

Excel **Advanced Skills**

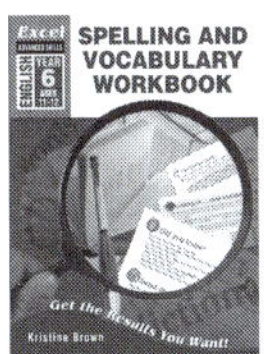

9781741252675

Excel **Handbooks & Guides**

9781864410617

9781741252637

Excel **NAPLAN*-style Tests**

9781741254181

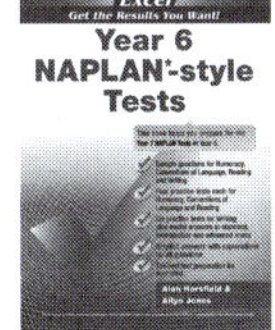

9781741253887

Vocabulary

Excel **Advanced Skills**

9781741252675

Excel **NAPLAN*-style Tests**

9781741254181

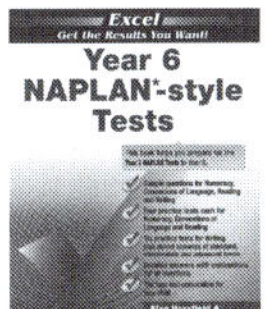

9781741253887

Grammar

Excel **Advanced Skills**

9781741254020

Excel **Handbooks & Guides**

Pascal's BASIC PRIMARY Grammar

9781864410600

Excel **NAPLAN*-style Tests**

9781741254181

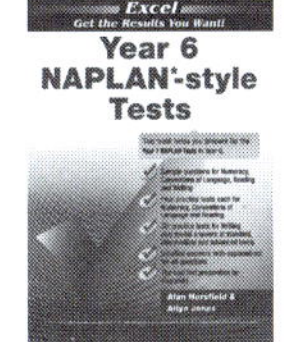

9781741253887

Punctuation

Excel **Advanced Skills**

9781741254020

Excel **NAPLAN*-style Tests**

9781741254181

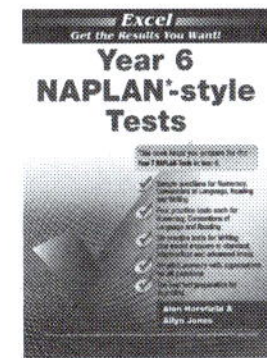

9781741253887

Writing

Excel **Advanced Skills**

9781741254051

Excel **Basic Skills**

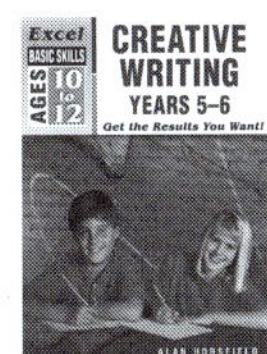

9781741250824

Excel **Handbooks & Guides**

9781741252835

Excel **NAPLAN*-style Tests**

9781741254181

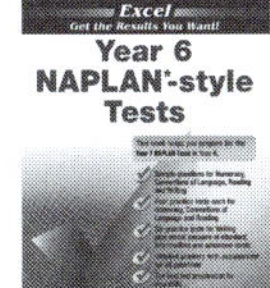

9781741253887

Question templates

Reading and comprehension

Q1–2 Literal: Answers to these questions are found directly in the text.

Q3–4 Inferring: Answers to these questions need to be worked out from clues in the text.

Q5–6 Evaluative: Answers to these questions rely on making judgements about information in the text and beyond the text.

Spelling

Q1–3 Misspelt words: In these questions, students use their understanding of spelling patterns and spelling rules to correct the spelling mistakes.

Q4 Prefixes: This question requires students to understand how adding a meaningful element to the beginning of a word changes its meaning.

Q5 Word families: In this question students use their understanding of base words, morphemes, prefixes, suffixes and etymology to create word families.

Vocabulary

Q6 Synonyms: In this question, students need to comprehend the meanings of words in context.

Q7 Etymology: This question requires students to use knowledge of word origins and word meanings to work out the answers.

Q8–9 Definitions: In these questions, students are required to demonstrate understanding of word meanings and usage in the context of the text.

Q10–11 Antonyms: In these questions, students need to understand synonyms and antonyms.

Grammar

Q12 Noun groups/Pronouns: This question deals with noun groups, pronouns and adjectival clauses.

Q13 Verbs/Verb groups: This question deals with aspects of verb groups, including tense and modality.

Q14 Adverbials: This question deals with adverbs, modal adverbs, prepositional phrases and adverbial clauses that tell time, place and manner.

Q15 Clauses/Connectives: This question deals with clauses in sentences and using connectives.

Punctuation

Q16–18 These questions deal with ways of punctuating sentences, e.g. adding capital letters, full stops, question marks, exclamation marks, commas, quotation marks, apostrophes, hyphens and parentheses.

Texts in context

Note: There is no marking grid for Unit C questions.

Q1–6 These questions deal with aspects of text, including:

Purpose and audience: These questions require students to recognise the purpose of a text (such as to inform, persuade or entertain) and the nature of its intended audience (the reader, listener or viewer).

Text structures and features: These questions require students to examine how a text is organised to achieve its purpose through, for example, sequencing, paragraphing, and comparing and contrasting.

Textual interpretations: These questions help students to analyse and compare texts and evaluate their effectiveness through, for example, language choices, imagery and point of view.

Get creative

Q7 This task requires students to create their own texts by adding to or responding to the models provided. Student responses will vary as this task is open-ended.

This icon indicates where students will need to use their own paper to answer the question.

Marking grid

Reading and comprehension	Literal	Literal	Inferring	Inferring	Evaluative	Evaluative
Question	1	2	3	4	5	6
Unit 1						
Unit 2						
Unit 3						
Unit 4						
Unit 5						
Unit 6						
Unit 7						
Unit 8						
Unit 9						
Unit 10						
Unit 11						
Unit 12						
Unit 13						
Unit 14						
Unit 15						
Unit 16						
Unit 17						
Unit 18						
Unit 19						
Unit 20						
Unit 21						
Unit 22						
Unit 23						
Unit 24						
Unit 25						
Unit 26						
Unit 27						
Unit 28						
Unit 29						
Unit 30						
Question	1	2	3	4	5	6

Marking grid

Conventions of language	Spelling					Vocabulary						Grammar				Punctuation		
	Misspelt words	Misspelt words	Misspelt words	Prefixes	Word families	Synonyms	Etymology	Definitions	Definitions	Antonyms	Antonyms	Noun groups/ Pronouns	Verbs/Verb groups	Adverbials	Clauses/ Connectives	Punctuation	Punctuation	Punctuation
Question	1	2	3	4	5	6	7	8	9	10	11	12	13	14	15	16	17	18
Unit 1																		
Unit 2																		
Unit 3																		
Unit 4																		
Unit 5																		
Unit 6																		
Unit 7																		
Unit 8																		
Unit 9																		
Unit 10																		
Unit 11																		
Unit 12																		
Unit 13																		
Unit 14																		
Unit 15																		
Unit 16																		
Unit 17																		
Unit 18																		
Unit 19																		
Unit 20																		
Unit 21																		
Unit 22																		
Unit 23																		
Unit 24																		
Unit 25																		
Unit 26																		
Unit 27																		
Unit 28																		
Unit 29																		
Unit 30																		
Question	1	2	3	4	5	6	7	8	9	10	11	12	13	14	15	16	17	18

READING AND COMPREHENSION

Text 1

RENEWABLE ENERGY—NEWS

STORING renewable energy

Wind and solar are Australia's great renewable energy resources and vital in the war against climate change, but when the wind doesn't blow and the sun doesn't shine what happens to electricity if there is not a backup supply? Electricity fails.

One solution to the need for a backup power supply is bigger and better batteries. Large-scale batteries can store electricity so that power supply does not fail.

Over recent years wind and solar technologies have rapidly improved along with the technology for large-scale battery storage options for the electricity generated by the sun and the wind. On 3 July 2017 Australian economist Ross Garnaut said, 'Australia's rich renewable energy resources could mean that Australia will emerge as the developed country with the lowest electricity costs … We have the opportunity to be the energy superpower of the low-carbon world economy.'

Large-scale battery technology is an important step towards achieving affordable energy and reducing greenhouse gas emissions.

1 Ross Garnaut believes that Australia
- **A** is an energy superpower.
- **B** has plenty of renewable energy resources.
- **C** is sunny and windy.
- **D** has a low-carbon economy.

2 Batteries can
- **A** provide rich renewable energy resources.
- **B** help the wind blow and the sun shine.
- **C** help Australia become an energy superpower.
- **D** store backup power.

3 Why are large-scale batteries needed?
- **A** because small batteries can't store renewable energy
- **B** so that electricity supply fails
- **C** because it's not always sunny or windy
- **D** because Australia is rich in renewable energy resources

4 Choose **all** that apply. Technological advances will
- **A** lead to a stable electricity supply.
- **B** make electricity cheaper.
- **C** ensure electricity supply will not fail.
- **D** ensure sun and wind supply enough energy.

5 The photo shows
- **A** a solar farm.
- **B** renewable energy batteries.
- **C** how to store renewable energy.
- **D** a wind farm.

6 Use evidence from the text to draw a conclusion about Ross Garnaut.
- **A** His opinion is generally respected.
- **B** Nobody believes what he says.
- **C** He does not know much about economics.
- **D** He is a newspaper reporter.

Answers and explanations on page 110

SPELLING

Rewrite the misspelt words in questions 1–3.

1 Australia has great renewible energy sources.

2 Wind and solar tecknology have rapidly improved.

3 Australia can be an energy supapower.

4 Add a prefix to this word from the text: **developed**. Then write a definition for the new word.

5 Write three words from the word family that includes **electricity**.

VOCABULARY

6 Use a dictionary that includes word origins. Explain the origin and meaning of this word from the text: **emerge**.

7 Circle the answer that has the nearest meaning to the underlined word.

There are battery storage options.

A opportunities B failures
C choices D losses

8 Choose the correct definition for this word from the text: **solution**.

A answer B response
C resolution D problem

9 Write a definition for this phrase from the text: **energy superpower**.

Circle the word that does **not** belong.

10 A resources B disadvantages
C reserves D assets

11 A fail B profit
C crash D collapse

GRAMMAR

12 Add adjectives to extend the noun group.

Wind and solar are .... resources.

13 Circle the verbs or verb groups in each sentence.

A Electricity can be stored in batteries so that power supply does not fail.

B The storing of electricity in batteries means that power supply does not fail.

14 Which sentence shows the most certainty?

A Wind and solar might improve people's lives.

B Wind and solar are likely to improve people's lives.

C Wind and solar improve people's lives.

D Wind and solar will definitely improve people's lives.

15 Circle the connective then underline the main (independent) clause in the sentence.

Wind is a great source of renewable energy when the wind is blowing.

PUNCTUATION

16 Circle the sentence that is punctuated correctly.

A Australia's power grid needs large-scale batteries.

B Ross garnaut is an Australian economist.

C Power can fail unless theres a back up supply.

Rewrite each sentence correctly.

17 australia has plenty of sun and wind

18 large scale battery storage is important for the future announced ross garnaut

Answers and explanations on page 110

Text 2

Farmers for climate action

Anika Molesworth

Anika's family has a sheep station in outback NSW. She divides her time between there and working as an agricultural researcher. Her research takes her overseas for field work in places such as the rice paddies of South-East Asia.

Anika is passionate about sustainable farming, environmental conservation and action to prevent further climate change. She is keenly interested in the conservation of natural and cultural heritage in farming communities and manages the Sustainable Farms program for the International National Trusts Organisation (INTO).

Anika has been an invited speaker and educator at international conferences dealing with agricultural sustainability and natural resources. She made a presentation at the United Nations Paris Climate Conference (Paris COP21—Conference of Parties). She hopes to inspire others to seek excellence in environmental and agricultural work.

Anika has received the following Awards: 2015 Young Farmer of the Year, 2017 NSW Finalist for Young Australian of the Year and NSW Young Achiever Award for Environment and Sustainability.

1. Text 1 in Unit 1A
   - **A** tells how to help the environment.
   - **B** gives subjective information.
   - **C** is a biography.
   - **D** gives the writer's opinion.
2. Text 2
   - **A** tells how to be a sustainable farmer.
   - **B** is a biography.
   - **C** describes an organisation.
   - **D** recommends climate action.
3. Choose **all** that apply. In Text 2 the writer includes
   - **A** a call to action.
   - **B** a set of arguments for a point of view.
   - **C** statements supported by evidence.
   - **D** strong opinions.
4. Find an acronym in the text. Write it on the line. ....
5. The writer of Text 1 in Unit 1A
   - **A** agrees with Ross Garnaut's statements.
   - **B** makes judgements about people.
   - **C** is opposed to large-scale batteries.
   - **D** presents different sides of an argument.
6. Anika Molesworth and Ross Garnaut are similar because they are both
   - **A** working towards sustainable farming.
   - **B** talking to newspaper reporters about climate action.
   - **C** working towards climate action.
   - **D** influential people in their chosen fields.

7. How do renewable resources help prevent climate change?

Answers and explanations on page 110

READING AND COMPREHENSION

Text 1

Ten charms for Babette

Babette sat on the edge of her suitcase, which was perched at the edge of a cliff. She held the novel with intense concentration. She tried to continue to read, knowing that any lapse in concentration would cause the ground beneath her feet to crumble. She dared not move, even so much as to scratch her nose which was itching fiercely. The itch was getting worse because of her inability to scratch.

She read on.

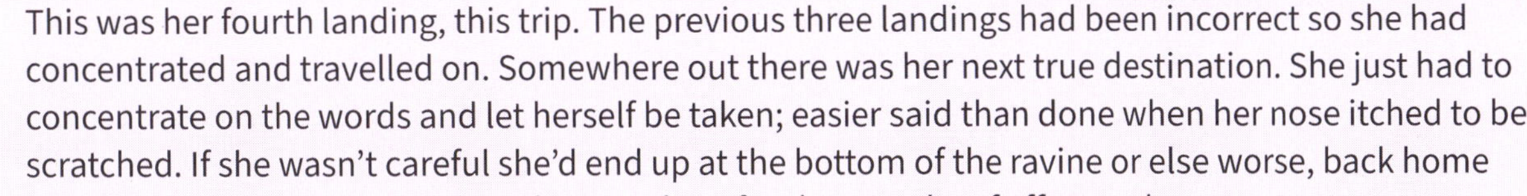

This was her fourth landing, this trip. The previous three landings had been incorrect so she had concentrated and travelled on. Somewhere out there was her next true destination. She just had to concentrate on the words and let herself be taken; easier said than done when her nose itched to be scratched. If she wasn't careful she'd end up at the bottom of the ravine or else worse, back home having lost the book and with nothing to show for the months of effort and no way to start over. She increased her concentration.

The suitcase held the charms she had collected so far. She had three for the first three chapters. She needed the next seven to complete the set. She had to get them all so she could win the challenge.

Chapter one had been easy but each of the subsequent charms had been more difficult to collect, with additional risks and challenges, and the destination for this fourth charm had eluded her so far and was making her frustrated. Her nose was threatening to take over her thoughts.

She read on.

1 How many charms did Babette need altogether?
- A six
- B seven
- C ten
- D four

2 What's in the suitcase?
- A nothing
- B charms
- C clothes
- D books

3 Why does Babette need to concentrate?
- A so she can travel on
- B so she can get to the bottom of the ravine
- C so she does not scratch her nose
- D so she can return home

4 Choose **all** that apply. Each chapter of the book
- A is more difficult to collect.
- B is more dangerous than the next.
- C takes her to a different destination.
- D allows her to collect one charm.

5 What is a likely series of events if Babette scratches her nose?

....

....

....

6 How does Babette travel?

....

....

Answers and explanations on page 110

SPELLING

Rewrite the misspelt words in questions 1–3.

1 She sat on the edge of her sootcase.

2 She dared not scrach her nose.

3 She increased her concentrashun.

4 Add a prefix to this word from the text: **complete.** Then write a definition for the new word.

5 Write three words from the word family that includes **thoughts**.

VOCABULARY

6 Use a dictionary that includes word origins. Explain the origin and meaning of this word from the text: **challenge**.

7 Circle the answer that has the nearest meaning to the underlined word.

The previous landings had been incorrect.

A complete B failures
C wrong D unsuitable

8 Choose the correct definition for this word from the text: **destination**.

A purpose B journey's end
C home D landing place

9 Write a definition for this word from the text: **crumble**.

Circle the word that does **not** belong.

10 A ravine B gorge
C abyss D hole

11 A subsequent B earlier
C following D next

GRAMMAR

12 Add adjectives to extend the noun group

The ____ ____ suitcase held Babette's charms.

13 Circle the verbs or verb groups in each sentence.

A Babette had to collect the fourth charm but it had eluded her so far.
B Collection of the fourth charm had eluded Babette so far.

14 Which sentence shows the most certainty?

A Babette thought she could be in trouble.
B Babette knew she was really in trouble.
C Babette thought she might be in trouble.
D Babette definitely worried that she might be in trouble.

15 Circle the connective then underline the main (independent) clause in the sentence.

She could end up back home if she was not careful.

PUNCTUATION

16 Circle the sentence that is punctuated correctly.

A Babette perched on her suitcase;
B She'd end up at the bottom of the ravine.
C She was'nt concentrating hard enough.

Rewrite each sentence correctly.

17 the first second and third charms had been fairly easy for babette to collect

18 babette knew she had to collect all the charms

Answers and explanations on page 110

TEXTS IN CONTEXT

Text 2

Favourite genres

Ruby: I love scary stories and thrillers. They are suspenseful and exciting. My heart races and I cannot put them down. I used to like monsters and aliens but now I find creepy humans are scarier than monsters. *Witches* by Roald Dahl was my favourite book when I was younger.

Ahmed: I still like *Witches* but now I like fantasy stories, such as Harry Potter, or mystery stories where there are clues to solve, but not detective or crime mysteries. I don't like horror stories. I get a feeling of dread the whole way through them because I know something bad will happen and I hate that feeling. Plus I yell at the characters 'Don't go in there!' but they always do and something bad happens to them. It's too predictable.

Ellen: I like that feeling of dread and the build-up of suspense in horror stories. I like all genres but my favourite genre is adventure or survival. Those stories could be true and that makes them really exciting, like *Hatchet* by Gary Paulsen, because I imagine myself in a character's situation.

Rina: I read anything and everything except animal stories. I usually find them too sad.

John: I like realistic stories—ones that could be true. Then I can empathise with the characters.

Ahmed: Realism is my least favourite genre. I like to get lost with characters in an imaginary world.

John: Realistic stories have credible characters that you can empathise with.

Ahmed: If the author has developed the characters well enough, I empathise with characters in all genres but I think fantasy and science fiction are the only genres capable of having really exciting plots.

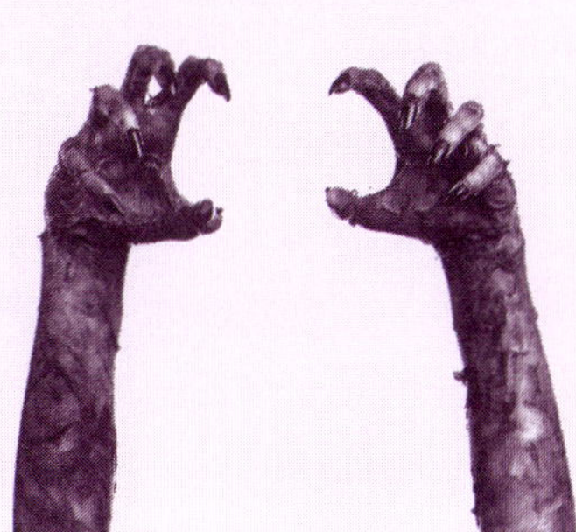

1 Which genre is Text 1 in Unit 2A an example of?
   A realism **B** horror
   C humour **D** fantasy

2 Choose **all** that apply. The children's purpose in Text 2 is to
   A persuade others to a point of view.
   B entertain.
   C share opinions. **D** inform.

3 In Text 2 which speakers would like the genre that goes with the illustration?
   A Rina **B** John **C** Ahmed
   D Ellen **E** Ruby

4 Choose **all** that apply. Empathising with characters is important to
   A Rina. **B** John. **C** Ahmed.
   D Ellen. **E** Ruby.

5 Which child in Text 2 is most likely to enjoy Text 1 in Unit 2A?
   A Rina **B** John **C** Ahmed
   D Ellen **E** Ruby

6 How are Texts 1 and 2 related?

....

....

....

....

Get creative

7 Explain your favourite genre.

Answers and explanations on page 110

READING AND COMPREHENSION

 Text 1

The disappearance

The magician stepped into the patch of light in the middle of the stage. The only things visible in the entire hall were his face and hands.

He announced that his finale for the evening would be to disappear. I felt people beside me squirm. Disappearing was pretty lame. It was just a trick with the lighting and a trapdoor under the stage. Up until that announcement the magician had been really impressive. The audience had oohed and aahed and gasped in amazement, but nobody was impressed when he announced that he would 'disappear'.

The magician remained silent for a few moments after his announcement, I guess to build tension and suspense. Then he counted backwards from ten and, by the time he reached four, he was gone; totally vanished from in front of our eyes—and not 'the lights went out' kind of vanished. The light continued to shine on the spot where he'd stood but he was, suddenly, no longer there.

There wasn't a sound to be heard in the hall. Then every light came on. The audience began clapping but that fizzled out when the stagehands appeared on stage, looking behind the curtains and scanning the audience.

The audience sat waiting for the magician to reappear. I felt confused and I heard murmurs from those near me who were also confused. Nobody seemed to know what was happening or what to do. Then a man came out and told everyone to remain seated until the magician could be located. He had indeed vanished into thin air.

1. Did the narrator think the disappearance was a trick?
   - **A** Yes, it was just a trick of lighting and a trapdoor.
   - **B** Yes at first but at the end, no.
   - **C** Yes, because the stagehands were part of the trick.
   - **D** No, because the magician was amazing.
2. After his announcement, it's most likely that the magician remained silent
   - **A** to prepare for his final trick.
   - **B** to make the audience watch him.
   - **C** to build suspense.
   - **D** so he could disappear.
3. The audience squirmed (line 4) because
   - **A** the magician announced his final trick.
   - **B** disappearing is a lame trick.
   - **C** the show was nearly finished.
   - **D** people were worried the magician would disappear.
4. What did people do when they were impressed by the magician?
   - **A** oohed and aahed
   - **B** squirmed
   - **C** murmured
   - **D** sat confused
5. The clapping fizzled out because
   - **A** the audience's hands grew tired.
   - **B** people did not want to clap for the stagehands.
   - **C** people realised there was nothing to clap for.
   - **D** a man told everyone to remain seated.
6. Overall, the narrator thinks the magician is
   - **A** unimpressive.
   - **B** pretty impressive.
   - **C** inspirational.
   - **D** amateurish.

Answers and explanations on pages 110–111

SPELLING

Rewrite the misspelt words in questions 1–3.

1 The magican stepped onto the stage.

2 He anounced that he would disappear.

3 The audiance began clapping

4 Add a prefix to this word from the text: **appeared**. Then write a definition for the new word.

5 Write three words from the word family that includes **visible**.

VOCABULARY

6 Use a dictionary that includes word origins. Explain the origin and meaning of this word from the text: **finale**.

7 Circle the answer that has the nearest meaning to the underlined word.

I guess he wanted to build <u>suspense</u>.

A suspicion B anticipation
C enjoyment D doubt

8 Choose the correct definition for this word from the text: **confused**.

A disorderly B puzzled
C indistinct D jumbled

9 Write a definition for this word group from the text: **fizzled out**.

Circle the word that does **not** belong.

10 A announcing B proclaiming
C declaring D renouncing

11 A impressive B awesome
C devastating D amazing

GRAMMAR

12 Add adjectives to extend the noun group.

The magician firstly performed a .... trick.

13 Circle the verbs or verb groups in each sentence.

A He announced his finale for the evening. It made people squirm.
B The announcement of his finale made people squirm.

14 Which sentence shows the most certainty?

A It seemed he had vanished into thin air.
B Maybe he had vanished into thin air.
C He really had vanished into thin air.
D He just possibly might have vanished into thin air.

15 Circle the connective then underline the main (independent) clause in the sentence.

Nobody was impressed when he announced that he would 'disappear'.

PUNCTUATION

16 Circle the sentence that is punctuated correctly.

A The spot where he'd stood was empty.
B There was'nt a sound in the hall.
C He was suddenly, no longer there.

Rewrite each sentence correctly.

17 wheres he gone asked oli

18 hed indeed vanished into thin air

Answers and explanations on page 111

TEXTS IN CONTEXT

 Text 2

Harry Houdini (1874–1926)

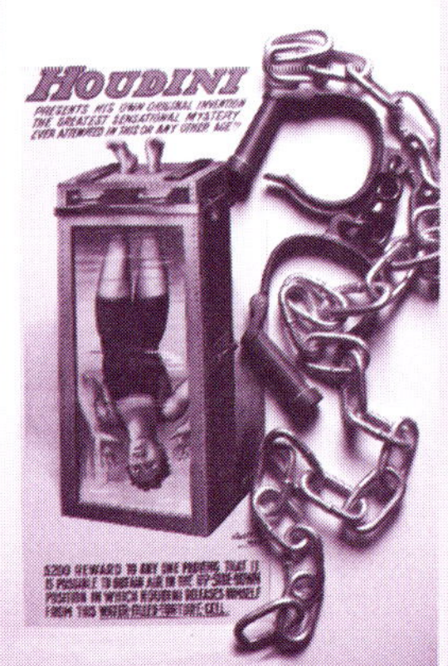

One of the most famous magicians of all time was Harry Houdini. He was famous as an escapologist. He performed stunts where he freed himself from handcuffs, straitjackets, chains and ropes to escape from locked jail cells and water-filled tanks. His performances were described as death defying and he kept audiences around the world on the edges of their seats.

One of Houdini's most famous stunts, and one he performed from 1912 until his death in 1926, was called the Upside Down or the Water Torture Cell. In this stunt he was hung upside down by his feet in a tank of water. He had to hold his breath under water for three minutes while picking the locks at his feet to escape from drowning.

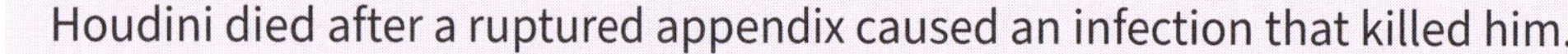

Houdini died after a ruptured appendix caused an infection that killed him.

1 The image used in Text 2 was created to

A inform. **B** persuade. **C** entertain.

2 What is the difference between Text 1 in Unit 3A and Text 2?

A Text 1 recounts events at a magic show while Text 2 advertises a performance.
B Text 1 is a story about a magician while Text 2 is a biography of a real magician.
C The magician in Text 2 does more death-defying tricks.
D Text 1 is written from the point of view of the narrator while Text 2 is written from the magician's point of view.

3 In Text 1 in Unit 3A, 'disappear' (line 7) is in inverted commas

A to highlight that it's amazing.
B because the name of the trick is 'the disappearance'.
C to highlight that it's true.
D because the writer does not believe the magician will disappear.

4 The phrase 'on the edges of their seats' in Text 2 (line 6) means that the

A performer was tense.
B audience could hardly wait to see what happened next.
C audience was keen to go home.
D seats were uncomfortable.

5 Which statement applies to both Text 1 in Unit 3A and Text 2?

A Some magicians are famous and others are not.
B Magicians rely solely on trickery.
C Magicians have the capacity to captivate audiences.
D Everyone loves a magic show.

6 Choose **all** that apply. Which statements are true in Text 2?

A Houdini was famous.
B Houdini died because he was a magician who did death-defying stunts.
C Houdini's expertise was in escaping from constraints and enclosures.
D Houdini could hold his breath for over five minutes.

7 Do some research into magic tricks and teach yourself how to do a number of them. Perform the tricks for an audience.

Answers and explanations on page 111

READING AND COMPREHENSION

Text 1

The castle

The castle stood on the rocky top of the hill. It had been owned by Tilda's ancestors in Scotland for hundreds of years. It now belonged to Tilda's father. It was exciting for Tilda to contemplate owning an actual castle. The problem was that the castle was too expensive for her dad to maintain. If he couldn't find a way to pay for its upkeep, he'd have to sell it. Tilda really didn't want that to happen.

This was her first visit to the castle. There was one staircase leading up. Tilda looked up towards the parapet, imagining what it would have been like to live in the castle in her ancestors' times. Her dad had told her that, centuries ago, when enemies were approaching the castle, a warning would have sounded and villagers from the surrounding fields would have rushed from their homes into the castle grounds behind the relative safety of the castle walls. (The stone staircase and the gaslights were added in the 1940s.) The Lord of the area was meant to protect the villagers. They were taxed to pay for the Lord's army as well as his lifestyle. It was how the world worked back then.

Tilda's dad wanted to turn the castle into a museum. Tilda hoped that tourists would pay to explore the castle and look at the displays of furniture, kitchen items, clothing, tools and weapons that her father had assembled. Meanwhile she would be spending the school holidays here. She hoped the castle wasn't haunted.

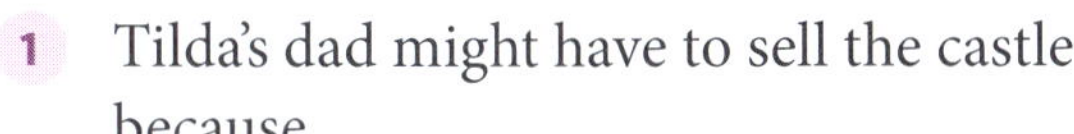

1 Tilda's dad might have to sell the castle because
- **A** his ancestors have owned it for hundreds of years.
- **B** it is not a museum.
- **C** he does not want to live there.
- **D** it's too costly to maintain.

2 Choose **all** that apply. Tilda was
- **A** excited about owning a castle.
- **B** worried about how to pay for its upkeep.
- **C** curious about life in the castle in the olden days.
- **D** angry about the Lord's taxes.

3 Why would people pay to visit the castle?
- **A** to see how people lived centuries ago
- **B** to see if ghosts were inside
- **C** to meet Tilda and her dad
- **D** to have a meal in the old kitchen

4 Choose **all** that apply. Which statements are true?
- **A** Tilda is afraid of ghosts.
- **B** Tilda does not want to live in the castle.
- **C** Tilda will only live in the castle temporarily.
- **D** Tilda does not get along with her dad.

5 In the past why were the castle grounds only relatively safe (lines 12–13)?
- **A** The castle walls were impenetrable.
- **B** There was a staircase that led enemies to the castle.
- **C** It was safer behind the castle walls than outside the walls.
- **D** Only relatives of the Lord were actually safe.

6 How does Tilda feel about her family history?
- **A** uninvolved
- **B** interested
- **C** not interested
- **D** proud

Answers and explanations on page 111

SPELLING

Rewrite the misspelt words in questions 1–3.

1 Tilda's ancesters were Scottish. ....

2 Villagers came from the surounding fields.

....

3 The museum held displays of furnature.

....

4 Add a prefix to this word from the text: **exciting**. Then write a definition for the new word. ....

....

5 Write three words from the word family that includes **centuries**.

....

VOCABULARY

6 Use a dictionary that includes word origins. Explain the origin and meaning of this word from the text: **centuries**.

7 Circle the answer that has the nearest meaning to the underlined word.

Tilda hoped that tourists would pay to visit the castle.

- A people who go to museums
- B people who travel around the world
- C people who visit places for enjoyment or culture
- D people who enjoy new experiences

8 Choose the correct definition for this word from the text: **taxed**.

- A charged a levy
- B tired
- C paid a toll
- D overexerted

9 Write a definition for this word from the text: **parapet**.

....

....

Circle the word that does **not** belong.

10
- A contemplating
- B considering
- C watching
- D imagining

11
- A expensive
- B dear
- C cheap
- D unaffordable

GRAMMAR

12 Add adjectives to extend the noun group.

Villagers rushed to safety within the

.... walls.

13 Circle the verbs or verb groups in each sentence.

- A When enemies approached, a warning sounded telling villagers to hurry inside the castle's walls.
- B The sounding of a warning, when enemies approached, told villagers to hurry inside the castle's walls.

14 Which sentence shows the most certainty?

- A Tilda was very excited.
- B Tilda seemed excited.
- C Tilda appeared to be excited.
- D Tilda should probably have been excited.

15 Circle the connectives then underline the main (independent) clause in the sentence.

Tilda hoped the castle wasn't haunted because that would be scary.

PUNCTUATION

16 Circle the sentence that is punctuated correctly.

- A The Lords army cost a lot.
- B It now belonged to Tilda's father.
- C The castle's upkeep was expensive

Rewrite each sentence correctly.

17 i hope the castle isn't haunted declared tilda

....

....

....

18 tildas ancestors were from scotland

....

....

Answers and explanations on page 111

TEXTS IN CONTEXT

Text 2

My Journal: Runnymede House, Hobart

Our class went on an excursion to Runnymede House in Hobart. The National Trust has restored Runnymede to what it looked like in the 1840s. The site is managed by the National Trust of Tasmania, which aims to preserve 'built heritage'. There is an entrance fee for members of the public.

Runnymede House was called Cairn House by Robert Pitcairn, the man it was built for in 1836. Pitcairn was born in Scotland but migrated to Tasmania. He was a lawyer and law reformer. He is famous because he campaigned vigorously against the cruel practice of convict transportation.

The second owner of the house was an Anglican Bishop, Francis Russell Nixon. He bought Cairn House in 1850 and renamed it Bishopstowe.

Whale watching has replaced whale hunting in Australian waters.

The third owner was a whaling captain, Charles Bayley, who purchased the house in 1864. He named the house Runnymede after his favourite ship. Bayley's descendants owned the house for 100 years and gave it to the National Trust in 1963. Whaling memorabilia such as scrimshaw is displayed in the house, along with a modern harpoon gun which exploded when it hit a whale. I am pleased that, nowadays, visitors to Australian waters photograph whales rather than kill them.

1 Text 2
- A gives information.
- B tells people to visit a house.
- C was written to entertain readers.
- D is a recount of a class excursion.

2 Who is most likely to read Text 2?
- A Pitcairn, Nixon and Bayley family members
- B the National Trust of Tasmania
- C students in the writer's class
- D visitors to the house

3 Choose **all** that apply. Which statements are true of both Text 1 in Unit 4A and Text 2?
- A Old homes have costly upkeep.
- B Old homes can show us how people lived in times gone by.
- C Old homes can be used as museums.
- D Some old homes are valued for heritage reasons.

4 Text 1 in Unit 4A gives the point of view of
- A Tilda and her ancestors.
- B Tilda and her dad.
- C Tilda.
- D the author and Tilda.

5 Which name for the house in Text 2 lasted the longest?
- A Bishopstowe
- B Runnymede
- C Cairn
- D Pitcairn

6 Both Text 1 in Unit 4A and Text 2
- A deal with old homes in Australia.
- B are about family relationships.
- C describe events in history.
- D include the concept of valuing 'built heritage'.

7 Investigate built heritage or natural heritage in your community. Write a report for class members to read.

Answers and explanations on page 111

READING AND COMPREHENSION

 Text 1

Warning

Dear Resident

The government will commence setting bait traps to target feral foxes in the Lockwood, Neering and Wellsford State Forests, commencing 3 July.

As the forests have boundaries with private land, neighbouring residents are warned that the traps will contain 1080 poison. This poison targets an animal's central nervous system and eventually kills it. Dog and cat owners need to keep their pets out of the state forests or muzzle their dogs when walking them through the forests.

Warning signs will be placed at all forest entrances.

The baiting program will last four weeks. The traps will be checked weekly until removal after four weeks. The effectiveness of the program will be assessed at that time.

NOTE: The European red fox is an introduced species in Australia. It is largely responsible for the decline in populations of native species, including the greater bilby, the bridled nail-tail wallaby, the green turtle and ground-nesting birds such as the night parrot. It also kills farm animals such as lambs.

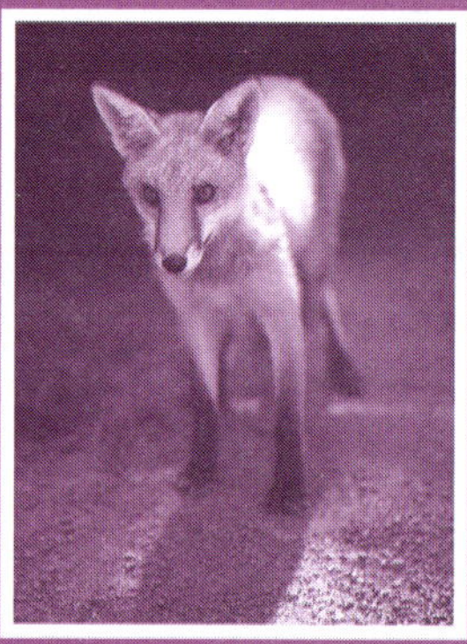

1 When taking a dog into the baited area, an owner needs to
- A muzzle the dog.
- B make sure the dog avoids foxes.
- C keep the dog on a leash.
- D read the warning signs at the entrance.

2 Who wrote the letter?
- A the Lockwood, Neering and Wellsford State Forests
- B the government
- C farmers
- D a dog owners' association

3 The 1080 bait will kill
- A European red foxes only.
- B any animal that eats it.
- C only the feral foxes.
- D all animals in the baited area.

4 How is the red fox responsible for native species' decline?
- A It is an introduced species.
- B Its favourite food is the bilby.
- C It hunts and kills smaller animals.
- D It is the cause of 1080 baiting.

5 Choose the best answer. A fox will kill
- A a variety of native animals.
- B bilbies, wallabies, turtles and night parrots.
- C cats, dogs and native animals.
- D all animals in the baited area.

6 Choose the best answer. This text
- A supports sheep farmers in protecting lambs.
- B does not support the use of 1080 poison because it kills pets.
- C urges people to complain about the dangers of 1080 poison.
- D supports the use of 1080 poison because foxes are a problem.

Answers and explanations on page 111

SPELLING

Rewrite the misspelt words in questions 1–3.

1 The govament agrees. ....

2 Check the forest boundries.

....

3 Residence need to be warned.

....

4 Add a prefix to this word: **assessed**. Then write a definition for the new word.

....

....

5 Write three words from the word family that includes **system**.

....

....

VOCABULARY

6 Use a dictionary that includes word origins. Explain the origin and meaning of this word from the text: **wallaby**.

7 Circle the answer that has the nearest meaning to the underlined word.

Baiting will <u>commence</u> soon.

A undertake B begin
C organise D eradicate

8 Choose the correct definition for this word from the text: **boundaries**.

A fences B limits
C borders D overlap

9 Use a dictionary. Write a definition for this noun group from the text: **State Forest**.

....

....

Circle the word that does **not** belong.

10 A decline B reduction
C improvement D dwindling

11 A help B abuse
C save D protect

GRAMMAR

12 Add adjectives to extend the noun group.

The government uses ....

.... traps in some places.

13 Circle the verbs or verb groups in each sentence.

A The Victorian Government will commence setting bait traps in state forests.

B The setting of bait traps in state forests by the Victorian Government will commence.

14 Which sentence shows the most certainty?

A You should make sure your pet is safe.
B You ought to make sure your pet is safe.
C You must try to make sure your pet is safe.
D You must make sure your pet is safe.

15 Circle the connective then underline the main (independent) clause(s) in the sentence.

Neighbouring residents are warned that the traps will contain 1080 poison.

PUNCTUATION

16 Circle the sentence that is punctuated correctly.

A Decline of native species' is a worry.
B the night parrot nests on the ground.
C 1080 poison targets an animal's central nervous system.

Rewrite each sentence correctly.

17 the european red fox is an introduced species

....

....

18 traps will be set on 3 july announced mayor wu

....

....

Answers and explanations on pages 111–112

Text 2

Poison is evil

DANGER
POISON

1080 is a poison used to kill animals. 1080 has been banned in some parts of the world but is still used in Australia. Countries that have banned 1080 have done so for animal cruelty reasons. Animals that eat 1080 die a slow and agonising death.

In Australia, 1080 kills more animals than just the target species. Wallabies and other herbivores can die when baited carrots and cereals are left out for feral rabbits.

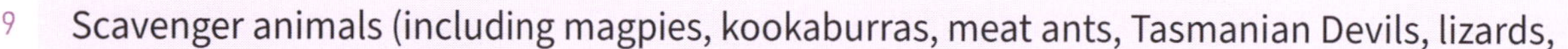

Scavenger animals (including magpies, kookaburras, meat ants, Tasmanian Devils, lizards, quolls, potoroos and dingoes) feed on the rotting carcasses of animals killed by the poison and they too become poisoned. In this way even insect-eating birds can die a painful death from 1080 poisoning.

Australian animal welfare groups have recommended a number of effective alternatives to 1080.

1 What is the purpose of Text 2?
- A to instruct how to use 1080
- B to give alternative viewpoints about 1080
- C to convince people to use 1080
- D to persuade against the use of 1080

2 Text 1 in Unit 5A is
- A a procedure.
- B informative.
- C persuasive.
- D a recount.

3 Text 2 includes
- A justification for baiting foxes.
- B information for and against 1080.
- C emotive words.
- D commands.

4 Choose **all** that apply. The writer of Text 2
- A presents opinions and reasons.
- B presents a judgement about countries that use 1080.
- C is opposed to 1080 use.
- D provides alternatives to 1080.

5 Which idea is **not** included in either Text 1 (Unit 5A) or Text 2?
- A People's actions cause animals to suffer.
- B People care about animal welfare.
- C Native animals face numerous threats.
- D Foxes have their place in Australia.

6 Choose **all** that apply. You can judge that the writer of Text 2
- A wants foxes dealt with humanely.
- B is concerned about animal suffering.
- C is happy that Australia might ban 1080.
- D is angry with animal welfare groups.

7 Why are feral animals a problem?

Answers and explanations on page 112

READING AND COMPREHENSION

 Text 1

Old-growth forests

Deforestation in Tasmania

Forests which have never been logged or cleared for roads are called old-growth forests. These forests are valued for their beauty as well as their importance in maintaining biodiversity. They contain very old trees. The old trees protect the ecosystem beneath their canopies. Old trees usually have hollows and dead limbs which are essential for the survival of many animals, including species such as gliders, possums, quolls, bats and owls. Some species of animals only live in old-growth forests.

As long ago as 2004 in NSW, the Department of Environment and Conservation reported that areas of old-growth forests 'now represent less than 10% of their original extent' (Natural Resource Management Advisory Series: Note 10).

In Queensland, environmental groups despair about the continued logging of old-growth forests (as well as other forests) and some estimates suggest that less than five per cent of Australia's old-growth forests remain.

Once old-growth forests are lost they are lost forever.

East Gippsland old-growth forest: For almost a decade (to 2015) up to one million tonnes of East Gippsland's forests have been made available for woodchipping each year for as little as nine cents a tonne. That is less than one dollar for a big eucalypt tree, some of which are hundreds of years old. Ancient forests are being clear-felled and turned into monoculture tree farms, destroying the biodiversity that has taken millions of years to evolve.

Source: www.wilderness.org.au/articles/goolengook-one-worlds-greatest-old-growth-forests-threatened

1 Hollows and dead limbs in old trees are essential for
- A old trees to survive.
- B the natural beauty of the forest.
- C the survival of many animals.
- D the Department of Environment and conservation.

2 The text states that woodchipping earns
- A nine cents for a big eucalypt tree.
- B one dollar per tree.
- C nine cents a tonne for old trees only.
- D nine cents a tonne.

3 Deforestation means
- A loss of forests.
- B replanting forests.
- C conservation of forests.
- D old-growth forests.

4 The inset quote (lines 16–20) was written by
- A the Department of Environment and Conservation.
- B the Queensland government.
- C a conservation organisation.
- D a government office.

5 Choose **all** that apply. Which statements are true?
- A Old trees protect the ecosystem beneath their canopies.
- B It's possible that less than 5% of Australia's old-growth forests exist today.
- C Logging a forest allows for greater biodiversity.
- D Plant and animal diversity in old-growth forests evolved over millions of years.

6 The text is
- A in favour of logging old-growth forests.
- B opposed to logging old-growth forests.
- C in favour of logging old-growth forests if it's managed properly.
- D in favour of logging old-growth forests because of the income logging provides by selling wood chips.

Answers and explanations on page 112

SPELLING

Rewrite the misspelt words in questions 1–3.

1 Old forests protect biodiversety.

2 Enviramental groups despair about logging.

3 Old trees provide a canipy.

4 Add a prefix to this word from the text: **management**. Then write a definition for the new word.

5 Write three words from the word family that includes **available**.

VOCABULARY

6 Use a dictionary that includes word origins. Explain the origin and meaning of this word from the text: **quoll**.

7 Circle the answer that has the nearest meaning to the underlined words.

Old-growth forests are very special.

A special forests B mature forests
C forests with big trees D ancient forests

8 Choose the correct definition for this word from the text: **biodiversity**.

A the differences between plants and animals
B the variety of plants and animals
C the numbers of plants and animals
D all living things

9 Write a definition for this word from the text: **monoculture**.

Circle the word that does **not** belong.

10 A quotes B forecasts C estimates D predictions

11 A magnificence B beauty C devastation D splendour

GRAMMAR

12 Add adjectives to extend the noun group.

The ______ ______ tree provided shelter for many animals.

13 Circle the verbs or verb groups in each sentence.

A Ancient forests are being cleared for monoculture tree farms. This destroys biodiversity.
B The clearing of ancient forests for monoculture tree farms destroys biodiversity.

14 Which sentence shows the most certainty?

A Ancient forests are really important.
B Ancient forests are pretty important.
C Ancient forests are probably important.
D Ancient forests are extremely important.

15 Circle the verbs or verb groups then underline the main (independent) clause in the sentence.

The old trees protect the ecosystem beneath their canopies ensuring the survival of other species.

PUNCTUATION

16 Circle the sentence that is punctuated correctly.

A The NSW Department of Environment and Conservation wrote a report.
B Less than five per cent of Australias old-growth forests remain.
C East Gippslands' forests have been woodchipped.

Rewrite each sentence correctly.

17 can we save australias old growth forests asked yelena

18 species such as gliders possums quolls bats and owls need tree hollows

Answers and explanations on page 112

TEXTS IN CONTEXT

Text 2

The Forest of Dread

Elon stood at the edge of the forest and listened. Nothing grew here but it seemed unnaturally quiet. The forest seemed to be holding its breath. He did not like this place. It was called the Forest of Dread for a reason. Only the pure of heart could traverse the forest unscathed. Many warriors had met their doom—judged by the forest.

To attempt to go through the forest was a risk but to go around would add three days to his journey. He could not afford the time. He and his brother had decided to split up, thinking that if Elon was to be doomed by the forest, at least Asher could survive to continue their task.

Elon believed he was pure of heart and, even though he was not certain the forest would judge him that way, he did not feel afraid. In any event he could not hesitate and must make his way through the forest as swiftly as he could.

He strode forth.

1 Find and write **five** words or phrases in Text 1 (Unit 6A) that are emotive.

....

....

2 Find and write **five** words or phrases in Text 2 that add atmosphere to the text.

....

....

3 Find and write **two** examples of personification in Text 2. (Personification is when human attributes are given to something non-human.)

....

....

4 Link the Text 2 words to their meanings.

traverse	walked purposefully
unscathed	travel through
dread	fear or apprehension
doomed	uninjured
strode	destined for something bad to happen

5 Choose **all** that apply. What does 'pure of heart' (line 5) mean?

- **A** free of guile
- **B** having no hidden motives
- **C** honest and open
- **D** guilty of wrongdoing

6 Use clues in the text to determine Elon's relationship with Asher. Choose **all** that apply.

- **A** They compete with each other.
- **B** They cooperate with each other.
- **C** They are equally responsible for decision-making.
- **D** Elon is braver.
- **E** Asher is braver.
- **F** Elon is pure of heart while Asher isn't.

Get creative

7 What might await in the Forest of Dread? Write the next paragraphs of the story.

Answers and explanations on page 112

READING AND COMPREHENSION

 Text 1

An ancestor's legacy

The scene in front of her was like something from Rose's worst nightmare. In the fog and the eerie dawn light she imagined lurking phantoms watching her. The bleak, biting cold only made it worse.

She sensed the arrival of Grace beside her and then she heard Grace's almost inaudible sigh. Grace had not wanted to come in the first place. She had argued that the abandoned cemetery would not be safe. It's a fool's errand she'd said and she believed no good would come of it. She had begged Rose to forget the whole thing but Rose had been determined.

Rose believed what she'd read in the ancient document she'd discovered in the crate of old dusty books in the basement under the stairs. Old Elijah, her great-great-grandfather, who'd died fifty years ago, had left an envelope addressed as follows: 'To the descendants of Elijah Wodendahl, may they prosper where he has failed. My legacy awaits those who have strength of character and mind.'

Inside the envelope was a cryptic note:

Seek the death stone
Marked for me.
And feel the place marked so.
In the depths there
Lays the key
To a second clue.

Rose did not know how many clues they had to work through but, swallowing her fear, she was now impatient to get started on the death stones. She turned on her phone torch.

1 Rose is Elijah's

- **A** granddaughter.
- **B** ancestor.
- **C** descendant.
- **D** friend.

2 What is a 'death stone'?

- **A** a stone used to kill someone
- **B** a stone cross
- **C** a stone that marks a gravesite
- **D** a decoration in a cemetery

3 Why is the note described as 'cryptic'?

- **A** It's a clue.
- **B** It was written in old-fashioned writing.
- **C** It includes instructions.
- **D** Its meaning is not clear.

4 What does 'get started on the death stones' (line 20) mean?

- **A** dig under them
- **B** read them
- **C** feel them
- **D** find one shaped like a key

5 Why is Rose keen to work through the clues? Choose **all** that apply.

- **A** She believes Elijah's words.
- **B** She wants to find her ancestor's legacy.
- **C** She hopes to prosper from her ancestor's legacy.
- **D** She enjoys solving mysteries.

6 Write Rose or Grace beside each adjective.

cautious	bold ....
loyal	determined ....
hopeful	confident ....
practical	cynical ....

Answers and explanations on page 112

SPELLING

Rewrite the misspelt words in questions 1–3.

1 She imagined lurking phantims.

2 She heard Grace's almost inaudable sigh.

3 My legacy awaits those who have strength of charactar.

4 Add a prefix to this word from the text: **patient**. Then write a definition for the new word.

5 Write three words from the word family that includes **audible**.

VOCABULARY

6 Use a dictionary that includes word origins. Explain the origin and meaning of this word from the text: **basement**.

7 Circle the answer that has the nearest meaning to the underlined word.

The cemetery was abandoned.

A unkempt B uncontrolled
C deserted D wild

8 Choose the correct definition for this word from the text: **prosper**.

A survive B live a long life
C win D be successful

9 Write a definition for this word from the text: **legacy**.

Circle the word that does **not** belong.

10 A task B errand
C mission D job

11 A clue B key
C hint D pointer

GRAMMAR

12 Add adjectives to extend the noun group.

In the .... light, Rose imagined phantoms.

13 Circle the verbs or verb groups in each sentence.

A Rose had discovered an old document. Written by Elijah Wodendahl, it gave Rose hope of a legacy.
B The discovery of an old document, written by Elijah Wodendahl, gave Rose hope of a legacy.

14 Which sentence shows the most certainty?

A In the fog she thought she imagined lurking phantoms.
B In the fog she wondered if she imagined lurking phantoms.
C In the fog all she could see were lurking phantoms.
D In the fog she seemed to imagine lurking phantoms.

15 Circle the verbs or verb groups then underline the main (independent) clause in the sentence.

Old Elijah had left an envelope when he died fifty years ago.

PUNCTUATION

16 Circle the sentence that is punctuated correctly.

A Old Elijah had died, fifty years ago.
B She heard Grace's almost inaudible sigh.
C Sh'ed discovered a crate of old dusty books.

Rewrite each sentence correctly.

17 it was like roses worst nightmare

18 the bleak biting cold only made it worse

Answers and explanations on pages 112–113

TEXTS IN CONTEXT

 Text 2

A Christmas Carol by Charles Dickens (1843)

… old Scrooge sat busy in his counting-house. It was cold, bleak, biting weather: foggy withal: and he could hear the people in the court outside go wheezing up and down, beating their hands upon their breasts, and stamping their feet upon the pavement stones to warm them. The City clocks had only just gone three, but it was quite dark already—it had not been light all day—and candles were flaring in the windows of the neighbouring offices, like ruddy smears upon the palpable brown air. The fog came pouring in at every chink and keyhole, and was so dense without, that, although the court was of the narrowest, the houses opposite were mere phantoms. To see the dingy cloud come drooping down, obscuring everything, one might have thought that nature lived hard by and was brewing on a large scale.

The door of Scrooge's counting-house was open, that he might keep his eye upon his clerk, who in a dismal little cell beyond, a sort of tank, was copying letters. Scrooge had a very small fire, but the clerk's fire was so very much smaller that it looked like one coal. But he couldn't replenish it, for Scrooge kept the coal-box in his own room; and so surely as the clerk came in with the shovel, the master predicted that it would be necessary for them to part. Wherefore the clerk put on his white comforter, and tried to warm himself at the candle; in which effort, not being a man of strong imagination, he failed.

1 How are Text 1 in Unit 7A and Text 2 similar? Choose **all** that apply.
- A They are both narratives.
- B They have bleak, cold, foggy settings.
- C Both stories are set in the olden days.
- D They both include old-fashioned terms.

2 In Text 1 (Unit 7A) a 'fool's errand' (line 6)
- A is an errand undertaken by a fool.
- B is an errand requested by a fool.
- C has no hope of success.
- D has to be completed in a cemetery.

3 Find and write the simile in Text 1 (Unit 7A).

....

....

4 Explain the different meaning of the term 'phantoms' in each text.

....

....

....

5 Choose **all** that apply. You know Scrooge is hard-hearted because he
- A locks the coal box.
- B won't let the clerk sit by the fire.
- C would dismiss the clerk if he asked for more coal.
- D doesn't trust the clerk.
- E provided the clerk with a small, dismal workspace.

6 The events in Text 1 (Unit 7A) have been put in motion by
- A Rose. B Grace. C Elijah.

The protagonist (main character) in Text 1 (Unit 7A) is
- A Rose. B Grace. C Elijah.

Get creative

7 Write a story with a cold, bleak, foggy setting.

Answers and explanations on page 113

 Text 1

It's too good to be true

A scammer is someone who pretends to have skills or knowledge that they really do not have and uses this pretence to swindle or con people into paying for fraudulent goods or services. Scammers make promises that are too good to be true yet lots of people fall for the scams, giving their money in the hope that the promises will come true.

Scams and scammers have been around for centuries. In ancient Rome (139 AD) guards killed the Emperor and offered the Empire for sale to the highest bidder. An offer of over a billion dollars in today's money was made but of course the guards could not sell an empire that did not belong to them. The guards responsible were executed.

In France in 1925 a scammer faked government documents and sold the Eiffel Tower to two scrap metal dealers who paid over $200,000. The scammer took the money to America where he continued his career as a con man.

Today internet scams are big business with people around the world losing billions of dollars to scammers. Advertisements lure investors with slogans such as 'get rich quick'. Some scams advise people that they have an overseas inheritance or a lottery win but to collect the money they must firstly pay fees into a foreign bank account. Of course, once the fees are paid there is no money to inherit or win. Other scams tug at people's heartstrings so they send money they think will be used to help someone in trouble. Some scammers tell you they can prevent your computer from crashing but you must act urgently and give them your passwords.

There is a well-known motto that serves as a warning for would-be victims of scammers: If something seems too good to be true it usually is.

 Text 2

Doc Dave's Premium Youthful Elixir

Do you want more out of life?

Would you like to be cured of all your ills, aches and pains?

Would you like to have a better concentration span?

Do you need more energy?

Youthful Elixir can give you all this and MUCH MORE. It cures the pain of headaches, coughs, colds, flu, toothache, arthritis, dementia, shyness, ageing, hair loss, warts, pimples, kidney trouble and depression. It also treats burns, kills germs and …

MAKES YOU FEEL EBULLIENT!

Try Doc Dave's Premium Youthful Elixir. Step right up. Pay for two bottles and get a third bottle absolutely FREE. Buy bottles for friends and family. Give a bottle to your teacher for the school holidays. He or she will come back to school a new person.

1 Tick the correct box to match the text to its purpose.

	Text 1	Text 2
to inform	☐	☐
to persuade	☐	☐
to entertain	☐	☐

2 Choose **all** that apply. People who fall for scams are likely to
- A begin new business adventures.
- B feel foolish.
- C lose money.
- D have regrets.

3 Choose **all** that apply. If scammers don't get caught they most likely
- A continue to run scams.
- B feel guilty and stop scamming.
- C develop bigger and better scams.
- D fall for scams themselves.

4 Do you need to pay a fee to collect a lottery win?
- A yes
- B no

5 Choose **all** that apply. In Text 1 you can judge that
- A the writer would never fall victim to a scam.
- B scamming is common.
- C scamming was more common in the past than now.
- D there are many different types of scams.
- E the internet is widely used by scammers.
- F scammers don't have a conscience.

6 In Text 2 the photo is of
- A the scammer who sold the Eiffel Tower.
- B Doc Dave.
- C an internet scammer.
- D someone cured by Doc Dave.

7 In Text 2 you can infer that the Elixir is a scam because
- A it promises to make your teacher a new person.
- B it makes promises that cannot be true.
- C the medicine cures shyness.
- D it promises to give you more out of life.

8 Which statement is correct?
- A Text 1 explains how to scam while Text 2 advertises a product.
- B Text 1 complains that scamming is wrong while Text 2 promotes a scam.
- C Text 1 defines what a scam is and Text 2 is a scam.
- D Text 1 tells people how to avoid being scammed while Text 2 explains a scam.

9 What is the purpose of asking the four questions at the beginning of Text 2?

....

10 What do people hope for when buying the Elixir in Text 2?

....

....

11 Give three reasons someone may fall for a scam.

....

....

....

12 Choose **all** that apply. You can judge that successful scammers
- A have good products and services to sell.
- B sound convincing.
- C are very persuasive.
- D believe in their products and services.
- E speak knowledgeably about their products and services.
- F understand human nature.

Answers and explanations on page 113

The incorrect word in each sentence has been underlined. Write the correct spelling of each word.

1 Scammers have <u>fraudulant</u> goods or services.

2 Scammers have been around for <u>centurees</u>.

3 Doc Dave's <u>elixer</u> makes you feel ebullient.

4 You can get a better <u>consentration</u> span.

5 Cure your <u>headake</u>.

6 Try it <u>absolutly</u> free.

7 Choose the correct answer to complete the sentence.

If something seems too good to be true, ………………… usually is.

A they B it
C them D we

8 In which sentence is **scam** used as a verb?

A The scam caught many people.
B He liked to scam the elderly in particular.
C It was a scam phone call.
D People caught up in the scam are very upset.

9 Which word or word group tells where the action happens?

In ancient Rome guards killed the Emperor and offered the Empire for sale.

A ancient Rome
B guards
C the Emperor
D the Empire

10 Add a describing adjective to extend the noun group.

People pay scammers for ………………… goods or services

11 Circle the verbs or verb groups in the sentence.

Some scams tug at people's heartstrings so they send money.

12 Which sentence shows the most certainty?

A It's a bit sad when people are scammed.
B It's sad when people are scammed.
C It's terribly sad when people are scammed.
D It's sad when innocent people are scammed.

13 Which adverbial correctly completes the sentence?

The scammer took the money ………………… .

A for America B by America
C to America D from America

14 Underline the main (independent) clause in the sentence.

A scammer is someone who pretends to have skills or knowledge that they really do not have.

15 Which sentence uses commas correctly?

A It cures headaches, coughs, colds, flu, toothache, arthritis, and dementia.
B It cures headaches coughs colds flu, toothache arthritis and dementia.
C It cures headaches, coughs, colds, flu, toothache, arthritis and dementia.
D It cures, headaches, coughs, colds, flu, toothache, arthritis and dementia.

16 Which sentence is punctuated correctly?

A Scams can tug at people's heartstrings.
B Scammer's trick people.
C A scam in ancient rome offered the Empire for sale.
D Scammer's are devious.

Answers and explanations on page 113

READING AND COMPREHENSION

Text 1

The magic lamp

Asifa and Tariq left the hustle and bustle of the crowded alleyways of the bazaar behind them as they stepped through the entrance to the shop.

'This is it,' said Asifa. She pointed at the map on her phone. 'This is where Dad was when he last messaged me. That was six hours ago.'

The shop was situated in the heart of the Grand Bazaar. Its interior was quieter and cooler than outside. The carpets draped all over the walls muted the cries of the hawkers outside, as well as the heat. There was no sign of a shopkeeper. The shop held all manner of treasures and oddments. Everything begged to be touched.

'Don't touch anything,' commanded Tariq. 'You'll break something for sure and we haven't any money to pay for breakages. We have to be careful with our money until we find Dad.'

Just then the shopkeeper appeared in front of them.

'Welcome,' he cooed. 'I have what you are looking for. I have everything your hearts desire. It is indeed lucky that I have found you.'

1 What are Asifa and Tariq trying to do?
- **A** buy gifts
- **B** escape from the heat
- **C** find Dad
- **D** hide from the shopkeeper

2 Outside the shop there are
- **A** carpets draped on the walls.
- **B** treasures and oddments.
- **C** noisy crowds.

Inside the shop it's
- **A** dark and busy.
- **B** quiet and cool.
- **C** empty and silent.

3 Why might the shopkeeper 'coo' (line 15) to Asifa and Tariq?
- **A** because he thinks they are frightened
- **B** to sound authoritative
- **C** to soothe and reassure them
- **D** to convince them to buy something

4 Choose **all** that apply. 'I have what you are looking for' (lines 15–16) might mean the shopkeeper
- **A** is proud of his shop and boasting.
- **B** has their dad.
- **C** is a good salesman.
- **D** is very confident in his ability as a shopkeeper.

5 Choose the best answer. The story is most likely
- **A** adventure.
- **B** science fiction.
- **C** realism.
- **D** humour.
- **E** romance.
- **F** horror.
- **G** mystery.
- **H** fantasy.

6 Who is older: Asifa or Tariq? Explain your reasoning.

....

....

....

Answers and explanations on page 113

SPELLING

Rewrite the misspelt words in questions 1–3.

1 The alleyways were crouded.

2 The hawker's cries were mutted.

3 The shop's interior was quiter than outside.

4 Add a prefix to this word from the text: **lucky**. Then write a definition for the new word.

5 Write three words from the word family that includes **breakages**.

VOCABULARY

6 Use a dictionary that includes word origins. Explain the origin and meaning of this word from the text: **bazaar**.

7 Circle the answer that has the nearest meaning to the underlined word.

The shop was situated in the heart of the Grand Bazaar.

A placed B inside
C located D hidden

8 Choose the correct definition for this word from the text: **alleyways**.

A shopping centres B roads
C narrow passageways D streets

9 Use a dictionary. Write a definition for this phrase from the text: **hawkers**.

Circle the word that does **not** belong.

10 A peddler B shopper
C hustler D hawker

11 A fete B bazaar
C marketplace D flea market

GRAMMAR

12 Circle the noun group to which **this** refers.

She pointed at the map on her phone. 'This is where Dad was.'

13 Circle the verbs or verb groups in each sentence.

A The shop was situated in the heart of the Grand Bazaar. Its interior was kept quieter than outside.

B The situation of the shop, in the heart of the Grand Bazaar, kept its interior quieter than outside.

14 Add a prepositional phrase (adverbial) to tell where.

Asifa and Tariq walked ....

15 Add a dependent clause of your own to complete the sentence.

Tariq said, 'We have to be careful with our money ....'

PUNCTUATION

16 Circle the sentence that is punctuated correctly.

A 'This is it,' said Asifa.

B 'Don't touch anything' commanded Tariq.

C 'Welcome, he cooed.'

Rewrite each sentence correctly.

17 this is where dad was said asifa

18 if we can find dad well be alright said tariq.

Answers and explanations on page 113

TEXTS IN CONTEXT

 Text 2

The tale of Aladdin

In this folktale a sorcerer tricks a young man, Aladdin, into stealing an old oil lamp from a cave of treasures, without telling Aladdin that he wants the lamp because it's magical. Aladdin gets trapped inside the cave but he is wearing the sorcerer's magic ring and when he wrings his hands in distress and accidentally rubs the ring, a genie appears. The Genie of the Ring helps Aladdin escape the cave with the lamp, evading the sorcerer.

Aladdin brings the lamp to his mother who attempts to clean it. Rubbing the lamp causes a genie to materialise; a genie more powerful than the Genie of the Ring. The Genie of the Lamp uses magic to create a palace for Aladdin and make him wealthy. Aladdin marries a princess, not telling her about his magic lamp.

The sorcerer hears of Aladdin's successes and realises that Aladdin must have the magic lamp. He tricks the princess into swapping a new lamp for Aladdin's old one and orders the Genie of the Lamp to steal Aladdin's palace.

Aladdin confides in the princess. Together they use the Genie of the Ring to slay the sorcerer. They regain the lamp and their palace.

The murdered sorcerer's brother seeks revenge. Disguised as a wise, old healing woman he ingratiates himself with the princess in order to move into the palace. The Genie of the Lamp warns Aladdin. Aladdin slays the sorcerer's brother and finally he and his princess can live happily ever after.

By Yasmin

1 The purpose of Text 2 is to
- **A** tell a story.
- **B** summarise a story.
- **C** explain a folktale.
- **D** persuade readers to read folktales.

2 Text 1 in Unit 8A and Text 2 both involve
- **A** a magic lamp.
- **B** the disappearance of a family member.
- **C** folktales.
- **D** the recounting of events.

3 Find and write an example of personification in Text 1 (Unit 8A).

....

4 The setting for Text 1 in Unit 8A is
- **A** Australia in modern times.
- **B** a shopping mall in an Australian town.
- **C** modern times in a foreign country.
- **D** olden times in the Middle East.

5 Which questions are raised in readers' minds after reading Text 1 in Unit 8A? Choose **all** that apply.
- **A** What has happened to Dad?
- **B** Why are Asifa and Tariq in the Grand Bazaar?
- **C** Will the children find their father?
- **D** Can the children trust the shopkeeper?

6 Choose **all** that apply. Themes in Text 2 include
- **A** love.
- **B** loyalty.
- **C** greed.
- **D** cunning.
- **E** betrayal.
- **F** trust.
- **G** trickery and deception.
- **H** survival.

7 What happens next in Text 1 (Unit 8A)? Continue the story.

Answers and explanations on page 113

READING AND COMPREHENSION

Text 1

Game on!

Erik could tell the children liked what Anne was demonstrating for them on the computer screen. Erik sat next to her, pleased as could be that his peers appreciated what he and Anne had created. This was an exciting moment after weeks and weeks of effort.

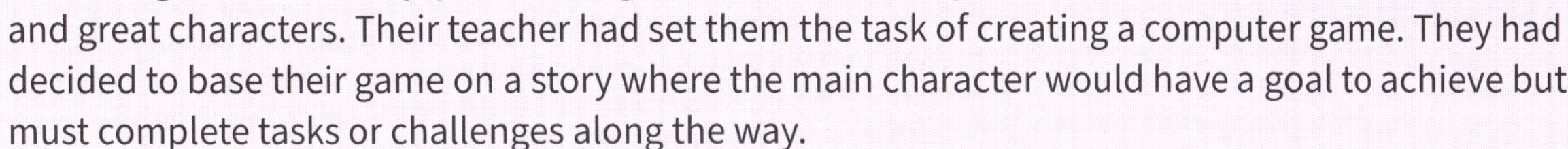

Erik believed that he and Anne made a good team. They each had a vivid imagination and enjoyed creating stories with exciting plots and great characters. Their teacher had set them the task of creating a computer game. They had decided to base their game on a story where the main character would have a goal to achieve but must complete tasks or challenges along the way.

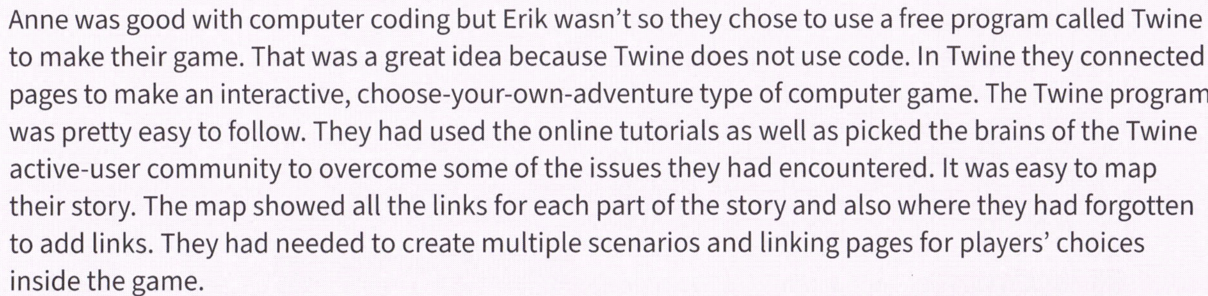

Anne was good with computer coding but Erik wasn't so they chose to use a free program called Twine to make their game. That was a great idea because Twine does not use code. In Twine they connected pages to make an interactive, choose-your-own-adventure type of computer game. The Twine program was pretty easy to follow. They had used the online tutorials as well as picked the brains of the Twine active-user community to overcome some of the issues they had encountered. It was easy to map their story. The map showed all the links for each part of the story and also where they had forgotten to add links. They had needed to create multiple scenarios and linking pages for players' choices inside the game.

Their game wasn't finished but what was done was really exciting. Erik was proud of their achievement so far and he knew Anne was too. He was keen to add more depth and complexity to their game and Anne had agreed with him.

1 The children are
- A in Erik's and Anne's home.
- B in school.
- C in Erik's home.
- D in Anne's home.

2 Erik and Anne had created a computer game based on
- A a book they had enjoyed.
- B a game on Twine.
- C their own adventure story.
- D a class novel.

3 Which statement is true in the text?
- A Twine is difficult to use.
- B The teacher told Erik and Anne to use Twine.
- C Anne is better with computers than Erik.
- D Erik has a more vivid imagination than Anne.

4 Choose **all** that apply. You can infer that Anne and Erik
- A enjoy working together.
- B don't have many friends.
- C enjoy playing computer games.
- D don't mind hard work.

5 Choose **all** that apply. As a team, Anne and Erik work
- A effectively.
- B collaboratively.
- C competitively.
- D respectfully.

6 Choose **all** that apply. You can judge that the children in Erik and Anne's class
- A are given exciting challenges.
- B have a teacher who expects a lot from them.
- C appreciate and respect each other's efforts.
- D are expected to work individually.

Answers and explanations on page 114

SPELLING

Rewrite the misspelt words in questions 1–3.

1 His peers appreshiated what he and Anne had created.

2 This was an exsiting moment.

3 They had encounterd issues.

4 Add a prefix to this word from the text: **connected**. Then write a definition for the new word.

5 Write three words from the word family that includes **exciting**.

VOCABULARY

6 Use a dictionary that includes word origins. Explain the origin and meaning of this word from the text: **community**.

7 Circle the answer that has the nearest meaning to the underlined word.

They had <u>encountered</u> problems.

A discussed B issued
C faced D solved

8 Choose the correct definition for this word from the text: **tutorials**.

A programs B games
C information D lessons

9 Use a dictionary. Write a definition for this word from the text: **plot**.

Circle the word that does **not** belong.

10 A multiple B numerous
C individual D many

11 A exciting B thrilling
C stimulating D boring

GRAMMAR

12 Circle the noun group to which **this** refers.

This was an exciting moment after their weeks and weeks of effort.

13 Circle the verbs or verb groups in each sentence.

A They chose Twine. That was a great idea.
B The choice of Twine was a great idea.

14 Add a prepositional phrase (adverbial) to tell when.

They had worked on the project .

15 Add a dependent clause of your own to complete the sentence.

They based the game on a story .

PUNCTUATION

16 Circle the sentence that is punctuated correctly.

A The plots' were exciting.
B Players' choices were limited.
C Their game was'nt finished.

Rewrite each sentence correctly.

17 erik and anne made a good team

18 the free progam was called twine

Answers and explanations on page 114

TEXTS IN CONTEXT

Text 2

Game on!

Top Games

TRENDING NOW | THIS MONTH | ALL TIME

FOREVER HOMES

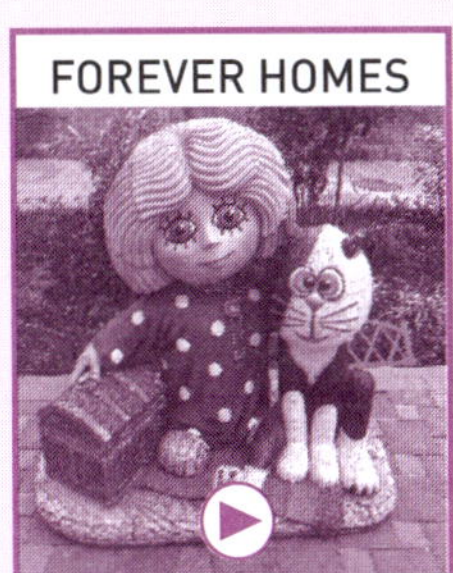

Press for free trial

ROBOT DESIGNER

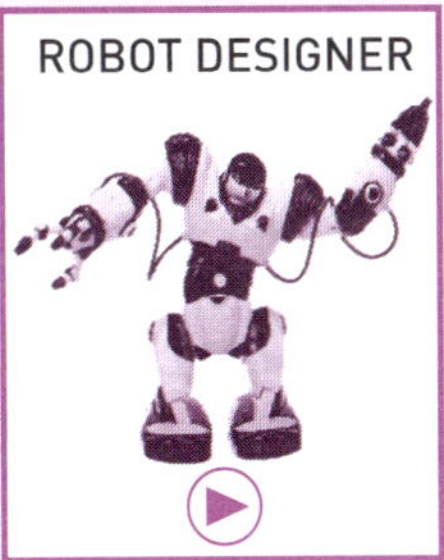

Press for free trial

LEGENDS OF RACING

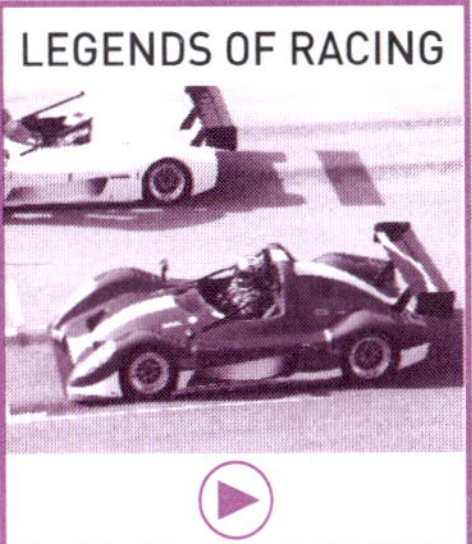

Press for free trial

ECO WARRIOR

Press for free trial

BATTLE FOR MARS

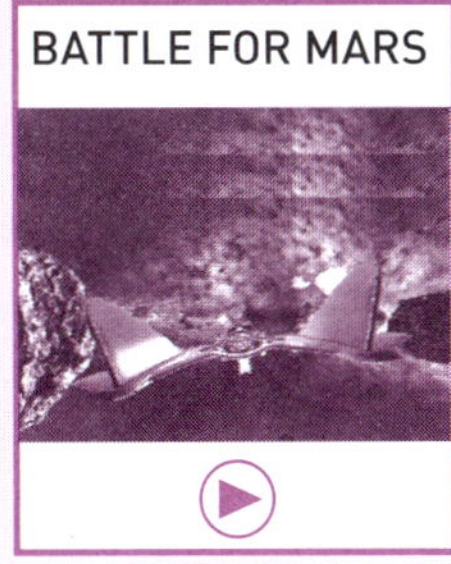

Press for free trial

Game reviews

#GAMERgirl *A fun challenge. Recommended if you like whales and dolphins.*

#Eriknocheatin' *My 'saved' game did not save and neither did my friend's. There's a glitch in the game. Please fix this. Good game otherwise.*

#I'mGame *I hate having to start over when you die. It's boring having to play through all the levels again*

#nightplayer *Gripping from the start. Travel through time solving mysteries. Family friendly.*

FREE TRIAL—LATEST VERSION

Try now!

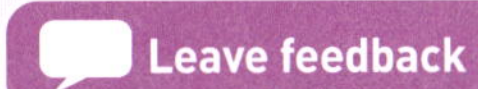

1 What is the purpose of Text 2?
   - A to sell computer games
   - B to promote computer games
   - C to solve people's gaming problems
   - D to explain how to use computer games

2 Choose the best answer. The audience for Text 2 is people who
   - A like to try free games.
   - B like to review games.
   - C are attempting to create their own games.
   - D play computer games.

3 Circle the correct answer in the brackets to complete the sentence.

   Text 1 in Unit 9A is written in the (first person / third person) from the point of view of (the narrator / Erik / Anne / both Erik and Anne).

4 Which statement is true of both Text 1 in Unit 9A and Text 2?
   - A Choose-your-own-adventure computer games are the most popular.
   - B There is a market for computer games.
   - C Computer games are immensely popular with people of all ages.
   - D Creating computer games is a challenge.

5 Might Erik or Anne have interest in the website in Text 2? Explain.

....

....

6 Which game listed in Text 2 would you choose to try and why?

....

....

7 Write a review of a computer game or computer activity.

Answers and explanations on page 114

READING AND COMPREHENSION

Text 1

Movie review: *Jurassic World*, rated M

This is an action movie set in modern times. Scientists have created dinosaurs using the DNA of extinct dinosaurs mixed with living animal DNA to create animals for a theme park called *Jurassic World*. I would love to visit this theme park, as would most young people, but I would be conflicted because I also think it's wrong to use animals for entertainment.

The movie has an exciting plot with lots of tense moments. The special effects are fantastic. The dinosaurs are amazing and the action sequences where the dinosaurs battle it out are spectacular. The dinosaurs are part animatronics, part CGI (computer-generated imagery) and part performance-capture technology.

The moral themes in the movie are fairly subtle. The male protagonist, Owen, has bonded with the raptors. He genuinely cares for their welfare while acknowledging that they are dangerous, wild creatures. He is brave and strong but kind-hearted, a perfect hero. He does not agree with others at the theme park that the dinosaurs are simply assets to be exploited. There is a message here about animal welfare but most viewers will not get it. There is also a message about scientists experimenting with DNA getting something they couldn't have imagined but this message will also mostly be lost in the excitement of the visual effects and the carnage.

The characters are pretty much stereotypes based on gender and good versus evil. The movie does have a brave female protagonist but she is also stereotyped in that she is career oriented and therefore has to be cold-hearted. During events in the film she learns that she has a heart after all.

I recommend this movie for people over the age of 12. It's worth watching for the excitement of the action sequences, especially if you love dinosaurs.

By Nadia, age 12

1 Nadia recommends the movie *Jurassic World*
- **A** only if you love dinosaurs.
- **B** only to 12-year-olds.
- **C** because its moral themes are fairly subtle.
- **D** because of its action sequences.

2 *Jurassic World*, the movie, is set in
- **A** the time of the dinosaurs.
- **B** modern times.
- **C** the future.
- **D** a real-life theme park.

3 Choose **all** that apply. The moral themes include
- **A** using animals for entertainment.
- **B** treating animals as assets rather than living beings.
- **C** experimenting with DNA.
- **D** the overuse of visual effects to show carnage.

4 What are **two** faults Nadia found with the movie?

5 Why would tension be important in the plot of an action film?

6 Choose **all** that apply. You can judge that Nadia
- **A** thinks most viewers would love to visit the *Jurassic World* theme park.
- **B** has no confidence in viewers being able to identify moral themes.
- **C** thinks the plot could have been more exciting.
- **D** was disappointed by the gender stereotypes.

Answers and explanations on page 114

SPELLING

Rewrite the misspelt words in questions 1–3.

1 The speshal effects are amazing.

2 The main male protaganist is Owen.

3 The main female character is stereotypt.

4 Add a prefix to this word from the text: **perfect**. Then write a definition for the new word.

5 Write three words from the word family that includes **acknowledging**.

VOCABULARY

6 Use a dictionary that includes word origins. Explain the origin and meaning of this word from the text: **animatronics**.

7 Circle the answer that has the nearest meaning to the underlined word.

The movie suggests that animals can be exploited.

A used B filmed
C killed D oppressed

8 Choose the correct definition for this word from the text: **genuinely**.

A warmly B truthfully
C sorrowfully D exclusively

9 Use a dictionary. Write a definition for this initialism from the text: **DNA**.

Circle the word that does **not** belong.

10 A subtle B understated
C blatant D obscure

11 A ethical B immoral
C moral D principled

GRAMMAR

12 Circle the noun group to which **this** refers.

Movie review: *Jurassic World*, rated M

This is an action movie set in modern times.

13 Circle the verbs or verb groups in each sentence.

A Using animals for entertainment is wrong because they suffer.

B The use of animals for entertainment is wrong because they suffer.

14 Add a prepositional phrase (adverbial) to tell when.

Jurassic World is set ....

15 Add a dependent clause of your own to complete the sentence.

The movie was exciting ....

PUNCTUATION

16 Circle the sentence that is punctuated correctly.

A Scientists experimented with dna.

B The Movie is called *Jurassic World*.

C The movie's worth it.

Rewrite each sentence correctly.

17 its an exciting film said nadia

18 nadia doesnt agree with the exploitation of animals

Answers and explanations on page 114

TEXTS IN CONTEXT

 **Text 2**

Zoos

Some people think it's wrong to keep animals in zoos because zoos are there to entertain people. I think that's wrong. Zoos provide more than entertainment. I think their main role is education. They show us the animals so that we can learn about them and want to protect them in the wild. I think zoos teach people about the importance of conserving animal habitats. They also inspire people to care for animals.

There are many fantastic zoos in Australia as well as in other parts of the world. They support conservation initiatives and help us learn more about various animal species. They ensure the animals are kept in conditions as close as possible to their natural habitats in the wild, including in the design of their enclosures. The best zoos provide enrichment activities for the animals so that they are mentally and physically stimulated.

Zoos can also be involved in breeding programs to ensure the survival of a species that may be endangered. Sometimes they even release animals bred in captivity to restock wild populations. I think that is wonderful.

My only concern about zoos is that in some parts of the world animals are not so well cared for. Sometimes they are kept in confined spaces and some animals are not provided with adequate medical care or even food. I think that those zoos are sad places for animals.

By Finn, age 12

The suffix *-osis* is commonly used for diseases or diseased conditions. For example:
Halitosis: bad breath
Thrombosis: where blood clots form in blood vessels
Tuberculosis: a disease of the lungs
Zoochosis: a mental condition affecting animals in captivity when they are bored, lonely and stressed

1 The primary purpose of Text 1 in Unit 10A is to
- **A** entertain readers and moviegoers.
- **B** persuade others to agree with an opinion.
- **C** present a personal opinion.
- **D** recount the plot of a movie.

2 The primary purpose of Text 2 is to
- **A** entertain.
- **B** persuade readers to agree with a point of view.
- **C** give an opinion.
- **D** inform.

3 Find and write **four** emotive words used in Text 1 (Unit 10A) that give a positive opinion about the movie.

....

....

4 Find and write **five** emotive words used in Text 2.

....

5 How does the inset box relate to the main text in Text 2?

....

....

6 What is the connection between Text 1 in Unit 10A and Text 2? 

7 Write a review of a film you have watched. 

Answers and explanations on page 114

READING AND COMPREHENSION

 **Text 1**

Aged care

Grandpa recently moved into residential aged care but he's finding it difficult to adjust to life in one room. He says his world has shrunk. I think he's shrinking too. Mum says it's because he doesn't move about very much so he's losing muscle and bone and getting smaller and shorter. I tell him he should go for a walk around his building every day but he's lost his confidence about going out on his own. He's happy to walk outdoors if one of us is there to walk with him. He has a walker to lean on but I guess he's become a bit afraid of falling over.

At Grandpa's aged-care facility the staff organise activities to try to help the residents keep mentally and physically healthy. They have exercise sessions with music. If you are not good on your feet you can do the exercises sitting in a chair, moving your arms and lifting your feet. They encourage people to go to the dining room for meals rather than eat in their rooms. This is also good socially because apparently it's healthy to interact with others and have a social network and connections, and to engage others in conversation.

The residence also organises activities to keep people's minds active. There's bingo and craft activities like collage and painting. People are encouraged to continue their hobbies.

There's a sing-a-long every Tuesday in one of the common areas with a guest musician or DJ. Lots of the residents attend those and seem to know all the words to the songs.

Mum says Grandpa will adjust in time and with our support.

By Nellie

1 Which statements are true based on information in the text?
- **A** An active mind and an active body are important for overall health.
- **B** Social engagement helps keep your mind active.
- **C** Hobbies and sports contribute to happiness and positive mental health.
- **D** It's impossible to exercise if you are confined to a wheelchair

2 Why do staff like residents to eat meals in the dining room?
- **A** You can have private conversations if you eat in your room.
- **B** There's less work for them when they don't have to carry meals to rooms.
- **C** People talk while they eat.
- **D** The food stays hotter.

3 What three difficulties might staff have at the aged-care residence?

....

....

4 What does it mean when Grandpa says 'his world has shrunk' (line 3)?

....

....

5 Which of the following sums up how Grandpa might be feeling at the moment?
- **A** optimistic and hopeful
- **B** lonely and unsupported
- **C** miserable and unfit
- **D** sad but hopeful

6 What do you think Nellie hopes for her grandfather? 

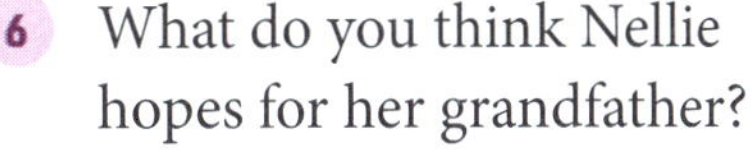
Answers and explanations on page 115

SPELLING

Rewrite the misspelt words in questions 1–3.

1 Grandpa is in residenshal care

2 Conversayshins are good for your health.

3 Ajusting to his new life will take time.

4 Remove the existing prefix and add a new one to this word from the text: **encourage**. Then write a definition for the new word.

5 Write three words from the word family that includes **connections**.

VOCABULARY

6 Use a dictionary that includes word origins. Explain the origin and meaning of this initialism from the text: **DJ**.

7 Circle the answer that has the nearest meaning to this word from the text: **facility**.
- A an aged-care residence
- B an ability to do something well
- C a place designed for a specific purpose
- D a piece of equipment

8 Choose the correct definition for this word from the text: **walker**.
- A a person who takes elderly people on walks
- B a device with a harness to help babies walk
- C a chair with wheels to support someone when walking
- D a cane or stick used to help a person walk

9 Use a dictionary. Write a definition for this word group from the text: **social network**.

Circle the word that does **not** belong.

10 A shrink B decrease C downsize D expand

11 A ignore B support C lift D help

GRAMMAR

12 Circle the word group to which **it's** refers.

I think he's shrinking too. Mum says it's because he doesn't move about very much.

13 Circle the verbs or verb groups in each sentence.
- A He enjoyed that exercise class once he settled in. It was great.
- B His enjoyment of that dance class, once he settled in, was great.

14 Add a prepositional phrase (adverbial) to tell where.

Grandpa has moved ....

15 Add a main clause to complete the sentence.

Because he doesn't walk much anymore

....

PUNCTUATION

16 Circle the sentence that is punctuated correctly.
- A Lets organise for friends to visit.
- B My sister loves mangoes (just like me).
- C Id have loved the music session.

Rewrite each sentence correctly.

17 how is the food asked mum

18 its not too bad but Id prefer to cook my own said grandpa

Answers and explanations on page 115

TEXTS IN CONTEXT

Text 2

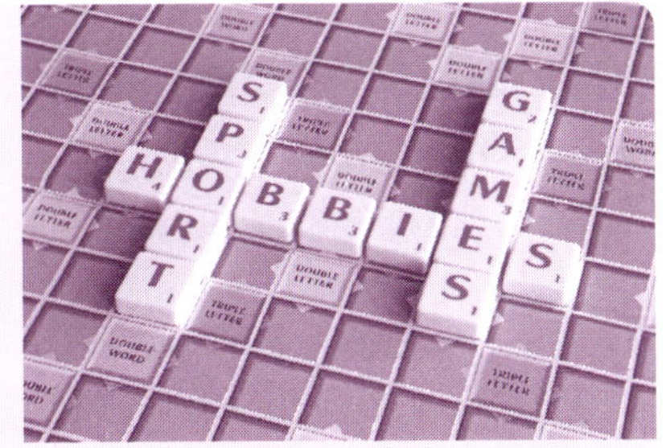

Sports can be hobbies

Rola: My family loves board games like Scrabble and Monopoly and Chess. We play all sorts. We have a cupboard full of games including card games. When we go on holidays we take the card games with us because they are easy to pack and carry. I love rainy Saturday afternoons at home when the five of us play games. Dad always says, 'Let's play indoor sports today.'

Hamish: We don't play board games in my home. Dad likes them but my stepmum doesn't and so we never play. She says they are a waste of time. Nan knits and crochets. Those are her hobbies. She's teaching me.

Kim: Knitting is boring. I get restless if I'm trapped indoors sitting down. Dad says I have ants in my pants. I don't have any hobbies but I love playing any sport.

Rola: A sport could be a hobby.

Hamish: I'm not sure a sport can be a hobby.

Rola: It probably can be. A hobby is something you do on a regular basis for fun.

Hamish: But hobbies are not really competitive like sport and they don't involve physical exertion like sport so they probably can't be called sports.

Rola: I think we maybe need to agree to disagree because I think people do sport for fun because they enjoy it and if they do it regularly then it is a hobby. And sport does not have to be competitive. I like ping pong and we play on our dining table at least once a fortnight and it's fun and it's our hobby. We keep score but it's not really competitive. Ping pong is an Olympic sport!

Carl: Some people might think hobbies are competitive. My grandmother enters cakes in cooking competitions. Dancing can be a sport because people compete in competitions and take it very seriously.

Kim: You can't just decide to call a sport a hobby or a hobby a sport. That doesn't make sense.

1. The purpose of the dialogue in Text 2 is to
   - **A** entertain.
   - **B** discuss.
   - **C** inform.
   - **D** describe.

2. Whose point of view does the title of Text 2 represent? Choose **all** that apply.
   - **A** Hamish
   - **B** Carl
   - **C** Rola
   - **D** Kim
   - **E** Rola's dad
   - **F** Hamish's stepmum

3. Who is most assertive in expressing opinions in Text 2? Explain.

   ....

   ....

4. Who provides the best arguments to support their opinions in Text 2? Explain.

   ....

   ....

5. What does 'ants in your pants' (line 10, Text 2) mean?

   ....

   ....

6. How do Text 1 in Unit 11A and Text 2 relate to each other?

   ....

   ....

   ....

7. Find out about another way of keeping healthy and write a text about it.

Answers and explanations on page 115

 Text 1

Maude Rose Lores Bonney, AM, MBE

Australia's aviation pioneers include Sir Charles Kingsford Smith from Brisbane, who achieved numerous aviation records including the first transpacific flight from America to Australia in 1928; Bert Hinkler from Bundaberg, Queensland, who made the first solo flight from England to Australia in 1928; and Nancy Bird-Walton from Sydney, who was given her first flying lesson by Charles Kingsford Smith, qualified for a pilot's licence at age 19 and later became known as the Angel of the Outback because she operated the Far West Children's Health Scheme, flying to outback areas not reached by the Royal Flying Doctor Service.

Belonging to this elite group of pioneering aviators is Maude Rose Lores Bonney. Taught to fly by Bert Hinkler, she became the first Australian woman to qualify as a commercial pilot. In 1932 Bonney became the first female pilot to circumnavigate Australia by plane. She was awarded the Qantas Trophy for 'the most meritorious performance by a Queensland pilot during 1932'.

In 1933 Bonney became the first woman to fly solo from Australia to England (against the prevailing winds) in a gypsy moth that she called *My Little Ship*. She flew a reverse course to that of Amy Johnson, the English pilot who had been the first female to fly solo from England to Australia. Bonney received an MBE from King George V in 1934, becoming the first female pilot to receive an MBE.

In 1937 Bonney became the first woman to fly from Australia to South Africa, a journey of 29 088 km that took 201 hours 45 minutes in her plane, *My Little Ship II*.

In 1939, at the outbreak of World War II, Bonney offered her services to the government as a flight instructor or ferry pilot but was told that the military had no use for female pilots. She retired from flying.

A gypsy moth plane, similar to Bonney's plane

1. Who taught Bonney to fly?
   - **A** Amy Johnson
   - **B** Nancy Bird-Walton
   - **C** Charles Kingsford Smith
   - **D** Bert Hinkler

2. Who was the Angel of the Outback?
   - **A** Maude Rose Lores Bonney
   - **B** Nancy Bird-Walton
   - **C** Charles Kingsford Smith
   - **D** Bert Hinkler

3. You can infer that Bonney was
   - **A** courageous and determined.
   - **B** timid but determined.
   - **C** brave and outspoken.
   - **D** very intelligent.

4. Why are the aviators mentioned in the text referred to as 'pioneering' (line 9)?

   ....

   ....

5. Why do you think the military had no use for female pilots in 1939?

   ....

   ....

6. How would you feel if you were Bonney and were told the military had no use for female pilots?

   ....

   ....

Answers and explanations on page 115

SPELLING

Rewrite the misspelt words in questions 1–3.

1 Bonney circimnavigated Australia.

....

2 The award was for meritorius performance.

....

3 Bird-Walton was the Angle of the Outback.

....

4 Add a prefix to this word from the text: **licensed** (adjective). Then write a definition for the new word. ....

....

5 Write three words from the word family that includes **reverse**. ....

....

VOCABULARY

6 Use a dictionary that includes word origins. Explain the origin of these postnominals from the text: **AM** and **MBE**.

7 Circle the answer that has the nearest meaning to the underlined word.

She flew <u>solo</u> from Australia to England.

A lonely B independent
C individually D single-handed

8 Choose the correct definition for this word from the text: **numerous**.

A few B many
C frequent D often

9 Use a dictionary. Write a definition for this phrase from the text: **prevailing wind**.

....

....

Circle the word or word group that does **not** belong.

10 A reverse B opposite
C backwards D sideways

11 A run-of-the-mill B elite
C exclusive D best

GRAMMAR

12 Circle the noun group to which **it** refers.

Australia has an elite group: aviators. Belonging to it is Maude Rose Lores Bonney.

13 Circle the verbs or verb groups in each sentence.

A Flying from Australia to England was against prevailing winds and broke a record for female pilots.

B The flight from Australia to England against prevailing winds broke a record for female pilots.

14 Add a prepositional phrase (adverbial) to tell where.

Bert Hinkler made the first solo flight to Australia ....

15 Circle the verbs or verb groups then underline the subordinate (dependent) clause in the sentence.

Nancy Bird-Walton, who was given her first flying lesson by Charles Kingsford Smith, qualified for a pilot's licence at age 19.

PUNCTUATION

16 Circle the sentence that is punctuated correctly.

A She flew for the Far West Children's health scheme.

B Maude Rose Lores Bonney was taught to fly by bert Hinkler

C Bonney received an MBE from King George V.

Rewrite each sentence correctly.

17 bonney was the first woman to fly from australia to south africa

....

....

18 bert hinkler was from bundaberg queensland

....

....

Answers and explanations on pages 115–116

TEXTS IN CONTEXT

Text 2

Milestones

In **1893** New Zealand became the first country in the world to grant women the right to vote in elections.

In **1894** the South Australian Parliament granted women equal rights to vote and to stand for elections in South Australia. These rights were a world first. The Constitutional Amendment was called the *Adult Suffrage Act*. The Bill was passed by 31 to 14 votes. The men who voted against women's right to vote mostly believed that women should devote their time to home duties.

Source: www.nma.gov.au/defining-moments/resources/womens-suffrage

In **1902** the Australian Federal Government granted (white) women the right to vote in Federal elections and the right to stand for election to the Federal Parliament.

Australia was the first country in the world to allow women to be elected to Parliament.

The first woman to stand for election in Australia was **Catherine Helen Spence** in Adelaide. She did not win the election but continued to work tirelessly throughout her life for women's suffrage (the right for women to vote) and on social and educational reforms.

At the celebration of her 80th birthday she said:

'I am a new woman, and I know it. I mean I am an awakened woman … awakened into a sense of capacity and responsibility, not merely to the family and household, but to the state: to be wise, not for her own selfish interests, but that the world may be glad that she had been born.'

Source: https://adelaidia.history.sa.gov.au/people/catherine-helen-spence

This portrait of Catherine Helen Spence is from the State Library of South Australia Portrait Collection, Ref B11192.

1 What is the purpose of the text?

2 The text assumes that readers understand terminology such as 'home duties', 'Bill' and 'elections'. Is this assumption reasonable, considering the audience?

3 Why do you think some words are bold in the text?

4 'that the world may be glad that she had been born' (line 21)

What do you think Spence meant by this?

5 Which of Bonney's personal characteristics (Text 1, Unit 12A) do you think Spence might have shared?

6 How does Text 2 relate to Text 1 in Unit 12A?

Get creative

7 Research a pioneer of your choice. Choose someone from any field that interests you and write a report.

Answers and explanations on page 116

READING AND COMPREHENSION

 Text 1

Save the Great Barrier Reef

The Great Barrier Reef is the world's largest coral reef system. It is home to over 400 species of coral as well as the fish, mammals, amphibians and birds that rely on it for their survival. The Great Barrier Reef is under threat because of climate change and the problems associated with climate change:

- Warmer oceans cause coral bleaching and ultimately large-scale coral die-off.
- Extra carbon dioxide is absorbed by the oceans, making them too acidic for coral to survive.
- Sea levels are rising because water expands when it warms. Rising sea levels flood land and cause sediment to flow into the sea, smothering coral.
- More severe and more frequent storms damage coral reefs.
- Increased rainfall leads to run-off (chemicals and other pollutants run into the oceans).
- Hotspots of warmer water occur throughout the reef system.

Turtle species rely on the Great Barrier Reef for their survival.

To save the Great Barrier Reef **we must drastically reduce greenhouse gas emissions** to limit climate change.

We **must** prevent further climate change and keep ocean temperatures from getting another two degrees higher or we will see the end of coral reefs—permanently and completely. Then the only place to see coral will be in a museum.

1 Why is the Great Barrier Reef under threat?

- **A** because too many animals rely on it for survival
- **B** because of climate change
- **C** because of the large coral reef system
- **D** because it is impacted by greenhouse gas emissions

2 Carbon dioxide makes oceans ....

....

3 Choose **all** that apply. Coral dies when

- **A** water is too warm.
- **B** water is too acidic.
- **C** turtles damage it.
- **D** water is polluted by agriculture.
- **E** rivers run into the sea.
- **F** sediment smothers it.
- **G** storms damage reefs.
- **H** greenhouse gases kill it.

4 Choose **all** that apply. The writer tells

- **A** why the reef needs to be saved.
- **B** how animals depend on the reef for survival.
- **C** why the reef is under threat.
- **D** which problems face the reef.
- **E** how to reduce greenhouse gas emissions.

5 Choose the best answer. The writer wants action to

- **A** control rising sea levels.
- **B** prevent storm damage to coral reefs.
- **C** control climate change.
- **D** save turtles.

6 The writer's worst prediction for the Great Barrier Reef is that ....

....

Answers and explanations on page 116

SPELLING

Rewrite the misspelt words in questions 1–3.

1 Amphibions such as turtles need the reef.

2 Pollutents run off land into the sea.

3 We must reduce greenhouse gas emishuns.

4 Add a prefix to this word from the text: **damaged**. Then write a definition for the new word.

5 Write three words from the word family that includes **reduce**.

VOCABULARY

6 Use a dictionary that includes word origins. Explain the origin and meaning of this word from the text: **species**.

7 Circle the answer that has the nearest meaning to the underlined word.

Sediment is smothering coral on the Great Barrier Reef.

A killing B dirtying
C covering D suffocating

8 Choose the correct definition for this word from the text: **threat**.

A danger B warning
C menace D evil

9 Use a dictionary. Write a definition for this noun group from the text: **climate change**.

Circle the word that does **not** belong.

10 A expands B decreases
C enlarges D swells

11 A increase B reduce
C lower D lessen

GRAMMAR

12 Circle the noun group to which **them** refers.

Carbon dioxide is absorbed by the oceans, making them too acidic for coral to survive.

13 Circle the verbs or verb groups in each sentence.

A Prevent further climate change. This is essential for the GBR.

B Prevention of further climate change is essential for the GBR.

14 Circle two adverbs.

We will see the end of coral reefs—permanently and completely.

15 Add a clause to complete the sentence.

When oceans become too acidic .

PUNCTUATION

16 Circle the sentence that is punctuated correctly.

A The Great Barrier Reef is the world's largest coral reef system.

B Fish, mammals amphibians and birds rely on the reef for their survival.

C Save the Great Barrier Reef,' said Jasmine.

Rewrite each sentence correctly.

17 the great barrier reef is under threat

18 storms sediment pollution and carbon dioxide hurt the gbr said sacher

Answers and explanations on page 116

TEXTS IN CONTEXT

 Text 2

Museum of natural history: marine extinctions

EXHIBIT 457: **Coral grown in captivity by Australian scientists**
Coral was once abundant on the Great Barrier Reef, Queensland, but became extinct in 2030 when the seawater temperature became too high for zooxanthellae to survive.

EXHIBIT 457

NB: Zooxanthellae are the algae organisms that live in coral, providing coral with nutrients and giving coral its colour. Coral bleaching occurs when zooxanthellae die or abandon their coral host.

EXHIBIT 7910: **Yangtze river dolphin**
The Yangtze river dolphin, or Baiji, likely became extinct in 2007. Loss of the species was rapid and attributed to loss of habitat caused by waterfront development, boat traffic and the construction of dams.

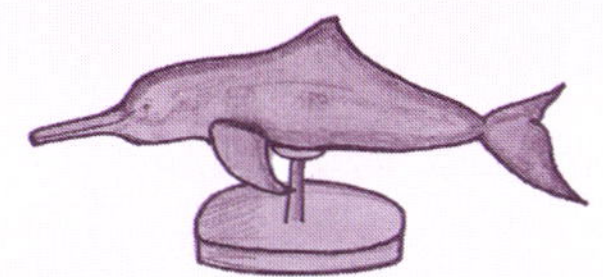

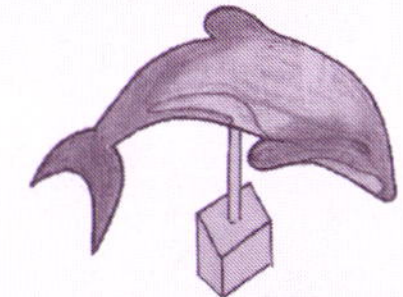

EXHIBIT 83201: **Maui's dolphin (subgroup of Hector's dolphin)**
This New Zealand dolphin species became extinct in 2025 mainly caused by drowning, as the dolphins regularly became entangled in floating fishing gear.

EXHIBIT D97745: **Taiji dolphin slaughter—a film**
The practice of using boats to drive dolphins into a cove in Taiji, selecting the younger dolphins for sale to dolphinariums or other forms of captivity, and butchering the rest of the pod for meat for human consumption, commenced in Japan in 1969 and led to the extinction of a number of dolphin species.

Press to play: The Cove at Taiji, Wakayama, Japan

1 Primary purpose

	Text 1 (Unit 13A)	Text 2
to persuade	☐	☐
to entertain	☐	☐
to inform	☐	☐

2 The audience for Text 2 is ....
....

3 What can you infer from the exhibit numbers in Text 2?

4 Find and write emotive words used in Text 2.
....
....
....

5 How does Text 1 in Unit 13A relate to Text 2? 

6 Choose **all** that apply. You can judge that the extinctions were all
- **A** related to climate change.
- **B** the result of problems with oceans.
- **C** caused by human activity.
- **D** preventable.

Get creative

7 Add an exhibit to the marine extinctions museum of the future.

Answers and explanations on page 116

READING AND COMPREHENSION

Text 1

A challenge

My sister and I love rock climbing. Our aunt owns an indoor climbing gym with artificial walls so we get to train there for free, which is very lucky for us. We've graduated to the tallest wall and our aunt changes the holds regularly to keep us challenged.

Our aunt is a competitive rock climber and has competed in events around the world. She teaches us the correct techniques and how to use all the safety equipment. My sister and I work as a team. We have learned to use ropes and anchors designed to catch us if we fall. We are 'free climbers', which means we use the equipment only for safety.

Rock climbers usually descend by their partners belaying them, although sometimes they may climb down or, if outdoors, can abseil or hike back down. Rock climbing is physically challenging. You need to be fit, flexible, strong and have good balance. You need really strong hands and fingers (as well as arms and legs) because you have to be able to support your whole bodyweight using just your fingers and hands. It is also a mentally challenging sport because you have to think and plan every grip and step. You really have to concentrate and you have to trust that your partner concentrates too.

Our aunt has promised to take us on her next outdoor climb with her rock-climbing club. We aim to travel the world climbing rocks, meeting other people who love rock climbing, and getting better and better at it. We aim to one day represent Australia in the youth team at the Lead Climbing Championships.

Liam, age 12

1 Choose **all** that apply. How do rock climbers get down from a climb?

- **A** They are belayed.
- **B** They abseil.
- **C** They crawl.
- **D** They climb.

2 Choose **all** that apply. Rock climbers need strong

- **A** teeth.
- **B** fingers.
- **C** hands.
- **D** legs.
- **E** arms.
- **F** toes.
- **G** sisters.

3 What does the title refer to?

- **A** physical challenge
- **B** mental challenge
- **C** physical and mental challenge
- **D** challenging relationships

4 You can infer that Liam is exceptional at the sport because

- **A** he aims to represent his country.
- **B** he says he loves it.
- **C** his sister is exceptional at the sport.
- **D** his aunt competes in the sport.

5 You can judge that Liam

- **A** loves the sport of rock climbing.
- **B** has a trusting relationship with his sister.
- **C** is often annoyed by his sister.
- **D** respects his aunt's rock-climbing expertise.
- **E** has a mutually respectful relationship with his aunt.

6 What has enabled Liam to become a rock climber? List **four** reasons.

....

....

....

....

....

Answers and explanations on pages 116–117

SPELLING

Rewrite the misspelt words in questions 1–3.

1 Our aunt is a competetive rock climber.

2 Use all the safty equipment.

3 Rock climbing is phisiclly challenging.

4 Add a prefix to this word from the text: **correct**. Then write a definition for the new word.

5 Write three words from the word family that includes **flexible**.

VOCABULARY

6 Use a dictionary that includes word origins. Explain the origin and meaning of this word from the text: **abseil**.

7 Circle the answer that has the nearest meaning to the underlined word.

She teaches us the correct techniques.

A safety grips
B physical skills
C the way the athlete performs
D specialised methods

8 Choose the correct definition for this word from the text: **regularly**.

A every week B infrequently
C often D sometimes

9 Use a dictionary. Write a definition for this word from the text: **artificial**.

Circle the word that does **not** belong.

10 A equipment B tools
C fingers D anchors

11 A challenging B demanding
C daring D defiant

GRAMMAR

12 Circle the noun group to which **it** refers.

We aim to travel the world, meeting other people who love rock climbing, and getting better and better at it.

13 Circle the verbs or verb groups in each sentence.

A We climb rocks. It is a challenging sport.
B Rock climbing is a challenging sport.

14 Circle two adverbs.

Liam and his sister work well and climb regularly.

15 Circle the verbs or verb groups then underline the dependent (subordinate) clause in the sentence.

Our aunt owns an indoor climbing gym with artificial walls so we get to train there for free.

PUNCTUATION

16 Circle the sentence that is punctuated correctly.

A We aim to represent Australia
B She competes in the Lead climbing Championships.
C Our aunt's a competitive climber.

Rewrite each sentence correctly.

17 you need to be fit flexible and strong

18 our aunts gym is fantastic exclaimed liam

Answers and explanations on page 117

Text 2

Easy Riders Cycling Club

HOME | GROUP NEWS | CONTACT US | EVENTS | JOIN | CONDUCT

Recreational group

- Enjoy cycling with like-minded people
- All welcome: current members aged between 11 and 86
- Ability levels: beginners to advanced/experienced

JOIN NOW

Regular local rides

- Every Saturday and Sunday
- 7 am spring and summer EDST/8 am autumn and winter
- 15 km or 25 km rides
- Meet in parking lot at Melrose Park, East Street
- 9 am: Meet at the entrance to the Gorse Hill Cycling Track

NB: This ride is more suited to beginners.

Midweek rides

- Wednesdays and Fridays 6 am: Meet in the parking lot at Melrose Park, East Street; experienced riders only
- Thursday 6 am beginner group: Meet at the entrance to the Gorse Hill Cycling Track
- For those of you who wish to compete or challenge yourselves, there are events such as Individual and time-trial events.

Find us online at www.easyriderscylingclub.com.au

1 Which person were the texts written in? Tick the correct box for each.

	Text 1 (Unit 14A)	Text 2
First person	☐	☐
Second person	☐	☐
Third person	☐	☐

2 Choose **all** that apply. Text 2 includes

A information. B commands.

C a recount. D warnings.

3 Does the club allow cyclists over the age of 86? Explain.

....

....

4 Choose **all** that apply. In Text 2 'more suited to beginners' implies that

A experienced riders won't enjoy this ride.

B the track is relatively easy.

C the pace is relatively easy.

D the distance is relatively easy.

5 Choose **all** that apply. You can judge that Easy Riders Cycling Club

A caters for a wide range of ability levels.

B encourages new members.

C looks after beginners.

D challenges experienced cyclists.

6 The photo is published to show

A club pride.

B club spirit.

C friendship.

D that club members are highly competitive.

E that the club does not want new members.

F that the club consists of friendly people.

7 Write an advertisement for an activity you enjoy doing with others.

Answers and explanations on page 117

READING AND COMPREHENSION

 Text 1

Mr and Mrs Smith Plumbing

My parents are plumbers. They also do roofing, drainage and gasfitting. They met when they were studying and they were enrolled in the same course. They did their apprenticeships with different employers but are now in business together. Their business is called Mr and Mrs Smith Plumbing.

Their names are not Smith. Mum's surname is Jankovic and she's a Ms not a Mrs, and Dad's surname is Thomsen, but they think Smith is a good name for the business as it is user friendly and easy to remember—better than Jankovic and Thomsen. It also helps customers realise that they can have a female plumber, which mum says lots of female customers like—especially if they live on their own. But mainly they named the business Mr and Mrs Smith because they saw a movie with that title. The movie was about a husband and wife who were assassins. I guess my parents enjoyed the movie. It starred some famous actors who don't look anything like my parents.

Mum specialises in roof and under-building work because Dad does not like heights or cramped spaces. He is the weightlifter of the team, although now with Workplace Health and Safety, there is very little heavy lifting. Also plumbers mostly don't use copper anymore as that is too expensive and has been replaced by plastics such as PVC.

Mum and Dad like their work. They get to do different things every week. They work indoors and outside. They keep fit and active. They especially enjoy renovations where they get to see a finished bathroom or kitchen and that gives them a lot of pride in their work. I haven't yet decided if I will join the family business and become a plumber too. I might.

By Jayda

1 Choose **all** that apply. Dad does not like

- A roof work.
- B under-building work.
- C cramped spaces.
- D heights.

2 Why is the business named Mr and Mrs Smith Plumbing?

3 Choose **all** that apply. The writer likes the business name because it is

- A user friendly.
- B easy to remember.
- C gender inclusive.
- D meaningful to Mum and Dad.

4 Choose **all** that apply. You can infer that Dad mostly does

- A gasfitting.
- B roofing.
- C heavy lifting.
- D renovations to kitchens and bathrooms.

5 Give **two** reasons why the business is likely successful.

6 Choose **all** that are true.

- A The writer is proud of Mum and Dad.
- B Mum and Dad have a sense of humour.
- C Mum and Dad will force the writer to become a plumber.
- D Dad thinks it's a bonus having a female plumber for the business.
- E Dad doesn't think women should be plumbers.

Answers and explanations on page 117

SPELLING

Rewrite the misspelt words in questions 1–3.

1 My parents are plummers.

2 They completed their apprentiseships.

3 They are now in bizness together.

4 Add a prefix to this word from the text: **decided**. Then write a definition for the new word.

5 Write three words from the word family that includes **customers**.

VOCABULARY

6 Use a dictionary that includes word origins. Explain the origin and meaning of this initialism from the text: **PVC**.

7 Circle the answer that has the nearest meaning to the underlined word.

They enjoy doing kitchen <u>renovations</u>.

A repairs B refurbishment
C redecorating D modernisation

8 Choose the correct definition for this word from the text: **enrolled**.

A registered B listed
C employed D studied

9 Use a dictionary. Write a definition for this word from the text: **apprenticeship**.

Circle the word that does **not** belong.

10 A cramped B confined
C restricted D overcrowded

11 A safety B danger
C protection D wellbeing

GRAMMAR

12 Circle the noun group to which **that** refers.

Plumbers don't use copper anymore as that is too expensive.

13 Circle the verbs or verb groups in each sentence.

A Renovating kitchens and bathrooms is what they enjoy most.

B The renovation of kitchens and bathrooms is what they enjoy most.

14 Circle the adverbial clause.

Mum met Dad when they were studying.

15 Underline the dependent clause.

The movie starred some famous actors who don't look anything like my parents.

PUNCTUATION

16 Circle the sentence that is punctuated correctly.

A Mum's surname is Jankovic.

B Workplace Health and Safety means workers are safer

C Their business is called Mr and Mrs Smith plumbing.

Rewrite each sentence correctly.

17 dads surname is thomsen said jayda

18 mums happy to work on the roof declared jayda

Answers and explanations on page 117

TEXTS IN CONTEXT

 Text 2

Discrimination

In Australia it's against the law to discriminate. There are many ways people can discriminate against others. People can discriminate on the basis of gender, religion, disability, ethnicity and age, among other things.

Sometimes people don't even realise they are discriminating according to Margaret Robertson, Chairperson of the Deafness Forum of Australia, 17 September 2004: 'Deafness has long been associated with stupidity, with incompetence, with difficulty and inconvenience. … 'She hears when she wants to' and 'She won't use a hearing aid' are all depressingly frequent accusatory statements made to or about the hearing impaired.'

There's a man who works in the same department as my aunty for the Automobile Association in the UK. His name is Douglas. Douglas's job is to take phone calls from people whose cars have broken down and want roadside assistance. He firstly listens to their car problems and tries to help them troubleshoot to get their cars going themselves. He's amazing at diagnosing what could be wrong with a vehicle and getting people under way again. But if they still need roadside assistance, he types all their details into the computer and sends a mechanic to help them. He loves his job of helping people. He has been doing it for 17 years and he is the best the company has ever had. He types in braille because he is blind.

Employment can provide people with disability with increased income, and with this, higher living standards and financial independence. Employment can contribute to a sense of identity and self-worth and has positive health impacts for some people with disability … Research has shown that workers with disability have higher rates of retention, better attendance and fewer occupational health and safety incidents than those without a disability. (www.humanrights.gov.au/publications/issues-paper-employment-discrimination-against-australians-disability/6-economic-and)

1 Which type of discrimination does Margaret Robertson specifically describe?

....

2 In Text 2 what workplace provision enables Douglas to do his job?

....

3 Which potential areas of discrimination do Text 1 (Unit 15A) and Text 2 relate to?

....

4 In Text 2 how might the Automobile Association feel about employing Douglas? Explain.

....

5 Circle the correct answers in the brackets to complete the sentence.
In Text 2 Margaret Robertson (whines / argues / proves) that people who are deaf are treated (fairly / appreciatively / unfairly).

6 Sometimes people with disabilities can't get jobs because of their disabilities. How would workplace discrimination have impacted Douglas's life?

....

Get creative

7 Survey children in your school about forms of discrimination they or their families may have experienced, in Australia or elsewhere. Report your findings to the class.

Answers and explanations on page 117

Text 1

BREAKING NEWS

ALIENS HERE—WAR IMMINENT!

By Rowena Hall

Last night a spacecraft crash-landed in a field 4.5 hours west of Sydney. Australian Federal Police and Defence Force personnel have cordoned off a two-square-kilometre area around the craft. As yet the craft remains sealed and according to leaked information there have been no sightings of alien beings.

In command of the operation is the Australian Army's Field Marshal Lydia Palmer. Speaking from command headquarters in Sydney, her face a blank page, she said, 'At this stage we don't know where the vessel came from or what it's doing here. We are keeping onlookers away from the site until we can confirm that it's safe. We will give the occupants of the vessel 24 hours to come out. If they emerge peacefully, attempts will be made to communicate. If nothing happens within the next 24 hours, we will presume the occupants died upon impact and proceed accordingly. The media is specifically requested to stay well clear and is prohibited from filming anywhere near the site. Breaching this request will result in the confiscation of camera equipment. Thank you for your patience.'

The Field Marshal will be joined, shortly, by representatives from other nations. Language and communications experts from major universities have also gathered near the craft in case their help is needed for communication attempts.

The eyes of the world are now focused on this once-peaceful field in the NSW countryside that now looks like an army camp.

Text 2

Where in the future?

My door handle rattled. Doreen tried pushing her way in but I'd tied the handle to a heavy chest of drawers and pushed all my furniture in front of the door to block it from opening.

'Go away!' I yelled

'What are you doing, Erin?' came Doreen's ugly, demanding voice.

'Homework. Let me concentrate.'

Silence from outside, then the handle rattled once more as Doreen pushed and thumped the door, grunting before walking away. I'd cop it later.

I wasn't doing my homework. I was working on something my grandfather had left for me in a box of his stuff. Grandpa was a genius. He was gone now, vanished like Mum, with no goodbye—just a box with a letter attached to the top, addressed to me. The letter said that if he disappeared too, then I was the only one who could help. In the box was a mysterious gadget along with instructions.

I was about to use the gadget for the first time.

1 In Text 1 the commander of the operation is from
- A the Australian Federal Police.
- B headquarters.
- C Sydney.
- D the Australian Army.

2 In Text 1 if aliens emerge, attempts will be made to
- A keep onlookers away.
- B communicate.
- C stay out of the safe zone.
- D talk to the media.

3 'her face a blank page' (lines 13–14)

What does this mean?
- A as if she didn't understand
- B deathly pale
- C as white as blank paper
- D No-one could read her expression.

4 In Text 1 the Field Marshal would prefer
- A for the aliens to be dead.
- B to fight the aliens.
- C peaceful communication.
- D other nations to be in charge.

5 In Text 1 what is the Field Marshal likely to do 'if nothing happens within the next 24 hours'?
- A bury the vessel because the occupants must be dead
- B attempt to open the vessel
- C attempt to destroy the vessel
- D leave the area because nothing will happen

6 Why are the media 'specifically' requested to stay out of the exclusion zone?
- A so they don't get in the way
- B to keep them out of harm's way
- C because the army might not want them to film events
- D to make sure they don't talk to the aliens first

7 Are the headings of Texts 1 and 2 effective? Explain.

....

....

....

8 Which features are evident in Text 1?
- A metaphor
- B quotation
- C by-line
- D emotive words
- E scientific theory
- F simile
- G eyewitness accounts

9 Choose **all** that apply. The term 'leaked information' (line 9) in Text 1 means information
- A given to the newspaper by someone not officially allowed to share it.
- B that people are not meant to know.
- C that is a secret.
- D that came from official sources.

10 In Text 2 what is the complication?
- A Erin is not doing her homework.
- B Grandpa left a mysterious box of stuff.
- C Doreen tries to push open the door.
- D Erin is about to use a mysterious gadget.

11 What evidence tells readers that Erin doesn't like Doreen? Choose **all** that apply.
- A She keeps Doreen out of her room.
- B Doreen makes her do her homework.
- C Grandpa and Mum are missing.
- D She knows she'll 'cop it later'.
- E She yells at Doreen.
- F She describes Doreen's voice as ugly, demanding and grunting.

12 Choose **two** answers. Give reasons for each choice. Erin is
- A brave.
- B foolish.
- C reckless.
- D independent.
- E curious.

....

....

....

Answers and explanations on pages 117–118

The incorrect word in each sentence has been circled. Write the correct spelling of each word.

1 Defence Force (personal) have cordoned off the area.

2 We saw (Feeld) Marshall Palmer.

3 Hopefully the (alians) are peaceful.

4 The (occupents) might have died on impact.

5 It was a (mysteryius) gadget.

6 (Furnature) blocked the door.

7 Choose the correct answer to complete the sentence.

Keeping onlookers away from the site, until .... is safe, is paramount.

A he　B he or she
C they　D it

8 In which sentence is **back** used as a verb?

A Back up the car.
B Scratch my back.
C I have a backache.
D When will you be back?

9 Which word group completes the sentence with the correct contraction of **could not**?

Grandpa .... have meant to disappear.

A couldnt　B couldn't
C could'nt　D coul'dnt

10 Which pronoun is implied in the gap below?

The letter said that if he disappeared too, then I was the only one who could help ....

A me　B it
C him　D that

11 Circle the verb or verb group in the sentence.

Grandpa had vanished into thin air.

12 Which sentence shows the most certainty?

A Grandpa seemed to have vanished.
B It's possible that Grandpa had vanished.
C Grandpa might have vanished.
D Grandpa had vanished.

13 Which adverbial correctly completes the sentence?

The furniture stopped the door ....

A with opening　B from opening
C to open　D about opening

14 Underline the dependent (subordinate) clause in the sentence.

We'll keep onlookers away until we can confirm that it's safe.

15 Which sentence uses commas correctly?

A Her voice was harsh, loud, and angry.
B He spoke quietly, hesitating before each word.
C 'We are, looking into it,' said the Field Marshal.
D 'Fetch the binoculars, and my night vision glasses,' said the Field Marshal.

16 Which sentence is punctuated correctly?

A 'What are you doing,' called Doreen.
B 'Its time for dinner,' said the cook.
C Erin was'nt doing homework.
D Grandpa'd vanished, like Mum.

Answers and explanations on page 118

READING AND COMPREHENSION

 **Text 1**

A conversation

I heard it on the grapevine, she said.
You're saving for a bike.
That'll cost you an arm and a leg.
I'm doing extra jobs, I said.
You can wash my car
she said
but don't cut any corners.
Piece of cake, I said,
it's not rocket science
but no need to pay me.
So I washed the car
and when I was done
she gave me $10 anyway
but she said,
Don't give up your day job.
Nan doesn't beat around the bush.
She's sharp as a tack.
She values hard work
and she's frugal with her cash.
Time is money
and waste not want not, she chants.
I take Nan with a grain of salt.
She's a real leg puller.
She's also the whole nine yards
and the best thing since sliced bread
whenever you need grandmothering.
She's loyal and loving
through thick and thin
and on that we see eye to eye.

1 When things cost 'an arm and a leg' (line 4) it means they are
- **A** affordable.
- **B** not worth buying.
- **C** a joke.
- **D** very expensive.

2 What does 'don't cut any corners' (line 8) mean?
- **A** Don't damage the car.
- **B** Do a thorough job.
- **C** Don't rush.
- **D** Work hard for your pay.

3 Why did the narrator say 'but no need to pay me' (line 11)? The narrator
- **A** had no intention of doing a satisfactory job.
- **B** was happy to wash the car for free.
- **C** already had enough money for the bike.
- **D** intended to do a cheap job.

4 'She's also the whole nine yards' (line 25)
- **A** is a compliment to the narrator.
- **B** means the narrator judges the car as a nine out of ten.
- **C** is a disrespectful remark about the grandmother.
- **D** means that the grandmother is a perfect grandmother.

5 'Don't give up your day job' (line 16) means
- **A** washing cars is a good day job for you.
- **B** you should wash the car more often.
- **C** don't expect to earn money washing cars in future.
- **D** get a job washing cars.

6 Choose **all** that apply. What is the relationship between the narrator and the grandmother?
- **A** They are loving.
- **B** They share the same sense of humour.
- **C** They make fun of one another.
- **D** The poet is disrespectful.
- **E** The poet takes advantage of the grandmother for money.

Answers and explanations on page 118

SPELLING

Rewrite the misspelt words in questions 1–3.

1 I heard it on the grapvine. ....

2 Nan does'nt beat around the bush.

....

3 She's frugel with her cash. ....

4 Add a prefix to this word from the text: **loyal**. Then write a definition for the new word.

....

5 Write three words from the word family that includes **science**.

....

....

VOCABULARY

6 Use a dictionary that includes word origins. Explain the origin and meaning of this word from the text: **grapevine**.

7 Circle the answer that has the nearest meaning to the underlined word.

waste not want not, she <u>chants</u>

A hums B yells
C recites D whispers

8 Choose the correct definition for this word from the text: **frugal**.

A not being wasteful with money
B spending money frivolously
C giving money away
D generous with money

9 Use a dictionary. Write a definition for this phrase from the text: **rocket science**.

....

....

Circle the word that does **not** belong.

10 A loyal B dependable
C trusty D disloyal

11 A appreciates B expects
C values D admires

GRAMMAR

12 What does **it** refer to in Text 1A on page 59?

I heard it on the grapevine, she said.

....

13 Rewrite this sentence in the past tense.

Nan is thinking about bicycles.

....

....

14 Underline the verbs then circle the adverbial clause.

She is the best thing since sliced bread whenever you need grandmothering.

15 Choose the best connective to complete the sentence.

I washed the car and (because / until / when / since) I was done, Nan gave me $10.

....

PUNCTUATION

16 Circle the sentence that is punctuated correctly.

A she's frugal with her cash.
B She's also the whole nine yards.
C Dont cut any corners.

Rewrite each sentence correctly.

17 although youve been given $10 you shouldnt spend it

....

....

18 in the morning after breakfast ill go to the bank

....

....

Answers and explanations on page 118

TEXTS IN CONTEXT

Text 2

Dr Evelyn Scott (1935–2017)

Dr Evelyn Scott was a First Nations Australian rights activist and a highly respected elder. Her grandfather was a South Sea Islander who was a slave in the sugarcane fields in Queensland.

Dr Scott became aware of discrimination against First Nations people in housing, health and employment in the 1960s in Townsville, North Queensland. She campaigned in favour of the successful 1967 constitutional referendum that gave the Commonwealth Government the power to make laws regarding First Nations Australians and to finally include them in the Census of the Australian population.

Dr Scott campaigned for land rights and social justice and was chairperson of the Council for Aboriginal Reconciliation between 1997 and 2000, working towards official government acknowledgement of the stolen generations.

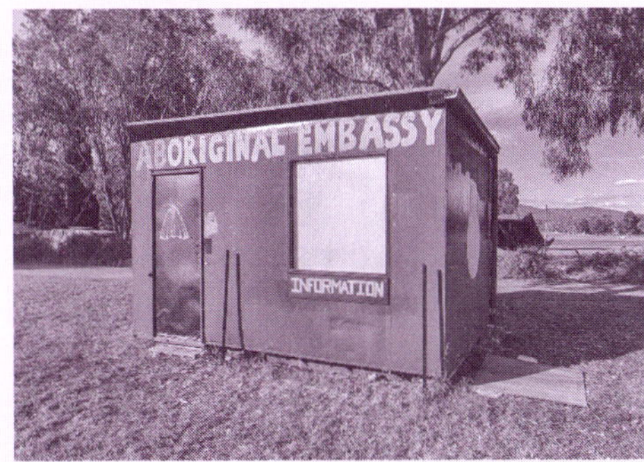

1972, Aboriginal Tent Embassy, Canberra, established in support of Aboriginal and Torres Strait Islander peoples' land rights

Dr Scott served as a Marine Park Authority Board Member from 1996 to 2007. Her goal was to protect the Great Barrier Reef and to promote the rights of traditional owners with the MPA Board in any decision-making about the GBR.

Dr Scott was 81 when she died. She was given a State Funeral by the Queensland Government.

1 The purpose of Text 1 in Unit 16A is to
  - A recount a conversation.
  - B entertain.
  - C describe a grandmother.
  - D persuade people to be kind to their grandmothers.

2 The purpose of Text 2 is to
  - A inform about the goals and work of an organisation.
  - B persuade people to support First Nations land rights.
  - C provide biographical information.
  - D entertain.

3 Choose **two** answers. The language in Text 2 is
  - A formal.
  - B personal.
  - C informal.
  - D distant.

4 Why was Dr Scott given a State Funeral?

....

....

5 Choose **all** that apply. Text 2 relates to Text 1 in Unit 16A because they
  - A are both about valued females.
  - B are both about people who have a good sense of humour.
  - C are both about respected elders.
  - D both advocate First Nations rights.

6 How might the grandmother feel about what is written in Text 1 (Unit 16A)?

....

....

....

Get creative

7 Write a poem about a member of your family.

Answers and explanations on page 118

READING AND COMPREHENSION

 Text 1

Book review: *Julie of the Wolves* by Jean Craighead George (1972)

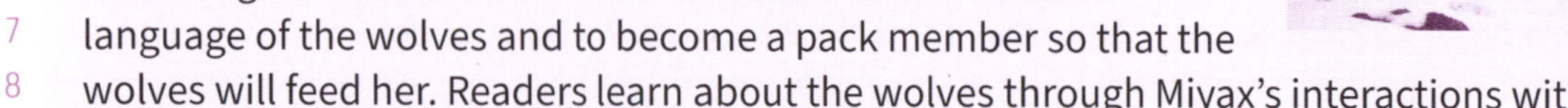

Alaskan Tundra Wolf

This is a very exciting adventure story. The setting is the tundra* on the North Slope of Alaska. The main character is Miyax. She runs away from home and becomes lost on the tundra. She uses her knowledge of wolves and her observation skills to learn the language of the wolves and to become a pack member so that the wolves will feed her. Readers learn about the wolves through Miyax's interactions with them. Flashbacks are used to tell readers about things that have happened in Miyax's past that are relevant to understanding her knowledge of nature and her behaviour in the present.

Miyax is a dynamic and well-rounded character. She has weaknesses as well as strengths. She makes mistakes that put her in danger but she learns from those mistakes in order to grow and develop. She learns to work in harmony with nature, following the old ways of her people. She learns also to question the influences of outsiders that are luring her people away from their traditional values. For example, she judges it wrong for white hunters to kill wolves for sport and for some of her people to make money from this type of tourism.

I really enjoyed reading about the magnificent and intelligent wolves in the story. The author uses her own in-depth knowledge about the animals and the setting. I also liked finding out about Miyax's people and their traditions. This is a gripping tale of survival.

Rating: 9/10, suspenseful and entertaining. I deducted one point because (spoiler alert) I was sad about Amaroq.

*A tundra is an area where the subsoil is permafrost (permanently frozen). Only the surface of the tundra thaws so it is impossible for trees to grow there. Only low-growing plants such as grasses, moss and lichen can survive.

1 The setting for the story is
- **A** Miyax's home on the tundra.
- **B** the frozen forests of Alaska.
- **C** cold and treeless.
- **D** a frozen place where nothing can survive.

2 What is a flashback?

....

....

3 You can infer that the complication in *Julie of the Wolves* occurs when Miyax
- **A** becomes a member of the wolf pack.
- **B** runs away from home.
- **C** learns the language of the wolves.
- **D** decides it's wrong to kill wolves for sport.

4 You can infer that Miyax's people are

....

5 The reviewer would define Miyax as
- **A** a tragic character who readers feel sorry for.
- **B** a heroic do-gooder.
- **C** a stereotyped female.
- **D** a complex character with both faults and good qualities.

6 After reading the review would you like to read *Julie of the Wolves*? Explain your answer.

....

....

....

Answers and explanations on page 118

SPELLING

Rewrite the misspelt words in questions 1–3.

1 Miyax learns the langwige of the wolves.

2 She uses her obsavation skills.

3 Flashbacks explain Miyax's behaviar.

4 Add a prefix to this word from the text: **relevant**. Then write a definition for the new word.

5 Write three words from the word family that includes **knowledge**.

VOCABULARY

6 Use a dictionary that includes word origins. Explain the origin and meaning of this word from the text: **tundra**.

7 Circle the answer that has the nearest meaning to the underlined word.

The wolves in the story were <u>intelligent</u>.

A brainy B gifted
C knowledgeable D clever

8 Choose the correct definition for this phrase from the text: **in harmony with nature**.

A not killing animals for sport
B living off the land as the traditional owners did
C living peacefully, sustainably and respectfully with all living things
D living harmoniously with others

9 Use a dictionary. Write a definition for this phrase from the text: **dynamic character**.

Circle the word that does **not** belong.

10 A unimpressive B magnificent
C incredible D amazing

11 A traditional B old-style
C customary D modern

GRAMMAR

12 Which pronoun is implied in the gap below?

She runs away from home and .... becomes lost on the tundra.

A he B she C it D they

13 Rewrite this sentence in the present tense.

In the story, Miyax made dangerous mistakes.

14 Choose the best connective to complete the sentence.

Miyax runs away from home and, (since / although / whenever / while) she has been out on the tundra before, she becomes lost.

15 Rewrite the sentence, adding the dependent (subordinate) clause: who we can empathise with.

Miyax is a flawed character and we worry about her.

PUNCTUATION

16 Circle the sentence that is punctuated correctly.

A Miyaxs past is told through flashbacks.
B I liked learning about Miyax's people.
C The tundra is in Alaska

Rewrite each sentence correctly.

17 although miyaxs interaction with the wolves is fascinating its a sad story

18 julie of the wolves was written by jean craighead george

Answers and explanations on page 119

TEXTS IN CONTEXT

Text 2

Is it sport to shoot animals?

The Google definition of sport is 'an activity involving physical exertion and skill in which an individual or team competes against another or others for entertainment'.

This definition implies choice. The people participating choose to be involved in competition with others. I don't think it is sport when animals are forced to physically exert themselves for the entertainment of humans. Animals such as horses and greyhounds don't get a choice. They are worked until they get injured or until they stop winning and then mostly they are put down.

Some people think that shooting animals is a sport. They shoot elephants and lions and wild pigs for their entertainment. They shoot animals from utes or helicopters. Some shooters, calling themselves 'big game hunters', travel to Africa and pay a guide to find them an animal to shoot, or they shoot lions bred in captivity specifically to be shot by hunters. (This is called 'canned hunting'.) I don't understand how someone can feel like a hero for killing any animal.

I also can't see how shooting defenceless ducks out of the sky is sport either. Shooters hide in reeds along waterways, scare ducks and other water birds into taking flight, then see how many birds they can shoot. Many birds are left wounded and suffer a slow painful death.

I like team sports such as hockey and basketball. I like individual sports such as cross-country, running and swimming. I like playing sport for fun, friendship and fitness.

There are thousands of different kinds of sports but any activity where an animal gets whipped or abused, worked to death or killed, can't be called sport.

1 The genre of *Julie of the Wolves* (Text 1, Unit 17A) is

A fantasy. **B** science fiction.
C horror. **D** adventure.
E humour. **F** historical fiction.

2 The purpose of Text 1 in Unit 17A is to

A persuade people to read a book.
B retell the story of *Julie of the Wolves*.
C give an opinion about a book.
D compare traditional and modern lifestyles.

3 The purpose of Text 2 is to ....

....

4 What is a 'spoiler alert' in Text 1 (line 20, Unit 17A)?

....

5 How does Text 2 relate to Text 1 (Unit 17A)?

....

....

....

6 Choose **all** that apply. Which words describe the writer's attitude to the topic in Text 2?

A angry **B** annoyed
C indignant **D** mystified
E judgemental **F** forgiving
G compassionate

7 Write a text about a topic on which you have strong opinions.

Answers and explanations on page 119

READING AND COMPREHENSION

Text 1

A person I admire

I admire my Uncle Ronnie. He is a paramedic for NSW Ambulance. He is on the front line of emergency care for sick or injured people. When he gets called out in an emergency he has to assess the person's health and make decisions about medical treatment on site and then get the person to the hospital safely and as quickly as necessary.

Ambulance operators help people in really stressful situations and save many lives. My uncle says it is a great job and personally very rewarding to know that you help people. Sometimes it is also a very distressing job, such as when he is called out to car accidents. He says these can be horrific but that he just has to concentrate on doing his job.

Another reason I admire Uncle Ronnie is for the fact that he has been an activist for social change for years. Ronnie first became an activist when his Council announced they were closing the library. He started a petition and then joined other people to march to the Council offices. They held up signs and banners that said 'Save our library' and 'Books matter'. They got their photo in the local newspaper too. In the end, the Council did not close the library. Ronnie says people have to stand up and be counted if they want to protect their rights and the rights of others.

Uncle Ronnie married his long-time partner, Elaine, on 8 February 2023. They got married in their backyard on a lovely sunny day. All their family members attended. Ronnie gave Elaine a mug as a wedding gift. It says, 'My husband is awesome'. That made me laugh.

By Scarlet, age 12

1. What is Uncle Ronnie's job?

   ....

2. Where did Uncle Ronnie get married?

   ....

3. Choose **all** that apply. You can infer that Uncle Ronnie has
   - **A** a good sense of humour.
   - **B** a job he is very good at.
   - **C** compassion for others.
   - **D** a sad life.
   - **E** an important job.
   - **F** a sense of social responsibility.
   - **G** an admiring niece.
   - **H** a loving family.

4. Why might Uncle Ronnie have protested to 'Save our library'?

   ....

   ....

5. Choose the best answer. You can judge that what Scarlet admires most about Ronnie is that he
   - **A** gave Elaine a funny mug.
   - **B** is a paramedic.
   - **C** is an activist.
   - **D** married Elaine.

6. What does Ronnie mean when he says that 'people have to stand up and be counted' (line 16)?

   ....

   ....

   ....

   ....

   ....

Answers and explanations on page 119

SPELLING

Rewrite the misspelt words in questions 1–3.

1 Ronnie is a paremedic. ……………

2 Ambulence operators help people.

……………

3 Ronnie was an activist to keep the libry open.

……………

4 Add a prefix to this word from the text: **involved**. Then write a definition for the new word.

……………

5 Write three words from the word family that includes **attended**.

……………

VOCABULARY

6 Use a dictionary that includes word origins. Explain the origin and meaning of this word from the text: **paramedic**.

7 Circle the answer that has the nearest meaning to the underlined word.

Ronnie is competent in an <u>emergency</u>.

A accident B contingency
C crisis D trauma

8 Choose the correct definition for this word from the text: **inspiration**.

A something that stimulates you to do better or be better
B something that is amazing
C a brilliant idea that is relevant for the times
D something that has a personal relevance to you

9 Use a dictionary. Write a definition for this word from the text: **activist**.

Circle the word that does **not** belong.

10 A awesome B fearsome
C amazing D tremendous

11 A behaviours B viewpoints
C opinions D attitudes

GRAMMAR

12 Which pronoun correctly completes the sentence?

When Ronnie gave Elaine the mug …………… said it was perfect.

A he B they C she D him

13 Rewrite this sentence in the present tense.

Ronnie will be nominated for a citizenship award.

……………

14 Choose the best connective to complete the sentence.

Ronnie believes in being an activist (because / however / when / while) an issue is close to his heart.

15 Rewrite the sentence, adding the dependent (subordinate) clause: that match their outdoor table.

We gave the couple some chairs as a wedding gift.

……………

……………

PUNCTUATION

16 Circle the sentence that is punctuated correctly.

A Uncle Ronnies a paramedic for NSW ambulance.
B Uncle Ronnie married his long-time partner, Elaine, in February.
C Ronnie is an inspiration to my Father.

Rewrite each sentence correctly.

17 ronnies wedding was in the backyard

……………

……………

18 ronnie and elaine were married in february 2023

……………

……………

Answers and explanations on page 119

TEXTS IN CONTEXT

Text 2

A good cause

Interviewer: Welcome to our segment on local heroes. Our guest today is Ron Costello. Good morning Ron.

Ron: Good morning Stella. Thank you for having me.

Interviewer: Ron, you've been nominated for a citizenship award. Please tell our listeners what the nomination is about and what it means to you.

Ron: The nomination is for my role in organising regular beach clean-ups in my community. Around 100 volunteers meet every month to clean up the beaches. We use social media to educate people about the environmental impact of plastic. We also visit schools to talk to the students. After each clean-up we tally the types of plastic and the volume of plastic in each category: straws, plastic bottles, fishing lines, polystyrene, plastic bags, cigarette butts, and so on, and we report the results to Council.

Interviewer: How did you first get involved in this cause?

Ron: I saw a need and I did something about it. People say I'm an activist and I am in the true sense of the word. I am acting to make my community a better place for everyone. It's a positive contribution to change. I couldn't sit at home and whinge about what was happening and how wrong it was. I had to get up and take action.

Interviewer: What are your plans going forward?

Ron: We plan to work with Council on ways to reduce the potential for plastic items to end up on the beaches. We are also working to engage local businesses and gather their support. For example, a 'no-straws policy' for cafes and takeaway food outlets.

1 The writer's purpose in Text 1 (Unit 18A) is to
- **A** offer a biography of a family member.
- **B** entertain readers.
- **C** persuade people to like the uncle.
- **D** give an opinion and support it with reasons.

2 The purpose of Text 2 is to
- **A** inform about plastic on beaches.
- **B** entertain listeners with ideas about community activism.
- **C** introduce listeners to an award nominee.
- **D** persuade listeners to join the beach clean-up events.

3 Choose **all** that apply. Ron's tone in Text 2 is
- **A** formal.
- **B** informal.
- **C** distant.
- **D** friendly.
- **E** conversational.
- **F** personal.
- **G** impersonal.

4 What is the 'need' (line 12) that Ron saw in Text 2?

....

5 Ron's role is to
- **A** say what the interviewer wants him to say.
- **B** offer insights into what it's like to be nominated for an award.
- **C** explain how to get nominated for an award.
- **D** offer firsthand experience.

6 What do Text 1 in Unit 18A and Text 2 have in common?

7 Write a text of your own with the title 'The person I admire'.

Answers and explanations on page 119

READING AND COMPREHENSION

 **Text 1**

Seeking the Magus

Crouching behind the large mossy roots of a tree, Helga observed the door. The lamp above it was on. That could mean that whoever lived inside was out and had left the lamp on because of an anticipated return after dark, or that the inhabitant was expecting a guest.

Helga grappled with her choices. Knock on the door and see if who she hoped lived in the tree answered her knock. Or wait until someone emerged and she could check that indeed she had found the correct address. Waiting was never easy for Helga. She was impulsive and impatient by nature, although recently she had learned the wisdom of pausing and thinking before acting.

If the address was correct and she had arrived before the Queen's Guard then there was hope. If the Queen's Guard had arrived ahead of her then it was already too late.

It was quiet in the forest. The door looked undisturbed. Was the lamp a signal of some kind? Did it signal that all was well? Or did it signal to beware? Had the Queen's soldiers turned it on to lure her in?

Helga was in a quandary. She wished Eamon was there to help her but he had needed to travel to Gorm, in the neighbouring kingdom, to rally support and had left Helga to seek out the Magus on her own. She knew he would return as fast as possible for their lives depended on it.

1 Eamon had travelled to ....

....

2 Had Helga found the correct address?

A yes **B** no **C** maybe

3 Who does Helga hope lives in the tree?

....

4 Choose **all** that apply. Helga inferred that the lamp could be on because

A the inhabitant forgot to turn it off.
B the inhabitant is expecting a guest.
C the inhabitant was out and expected to return after dark.
D the inhabitant is in bed.
E it was a signal of some kind.
F it was a trap.

5 'Helga was in a quandary' means that

A she did not want to act alone.
B she wished Eamon could help her.
C she couldn't decide what to do.
D she was seeking the Magus on her own.

6 If Helga was too late what might have happened?

A The Queen's Guard had captured Eamon.
B Eamon had arrived in Gorm ahead of her.
C The Queen's Guard had found the Magus before her.
D She'd learned patience too late.

Answers and explanations on page 119

SPELLING

Rewrite the misspelt words in questions 1–3.

1 They anticapated returning after dark.

2 She was impayshent by nature.

3 The gards might be nearby.

4 Add a prefix to this word from the text: **disturbed**. Then write a definition for the new word.

5 Write three words from the word family that includes **neighbouring**.

VOCABULARY

6 Use a dictionary that includes word origins. Explain the origin and meaning of this word from the text: **magus**.

7 Circle the answer that has the nearest meaning to the underlined word.

She could wait until someone emerged.

A appeared B arose
C came out D evolved

8 Choose the correct definition for this word from the text: **grappled**.

A wrestled with someone or something
B tried to overcome a problem
C tried to overcome an opponent
D hooked something and got hold of it

9 Use a dictionary. Write a definition for this word from the text: **impulsive**.

Circle the word that does **not** belong.

10 A wisdom B caution
C knowledge D intelligence

11 A compel B lure
C entice D bait

GRAMMAR

12 Which pronoun correctly completes the sentence?

Waiting was never easy for Helga. .... was impulsive and impatient.

A He B They C We D She

13 Rewrite this sentence in the present tense.

Helga was looking at the door.

14 Circle the adverbial clause.

She knew he would return as fast as possible for their lives depended on it.

15 Choose the best connective to complete the sentence.

She knew he'd be quick (whenever / however / when / because) their lives depended on it.

PUNCTUATION

16 Circle the sentence that is punctuated correctly.

A She wished eamon was there.
B Had the Queens' Guard arrived first?
C Did the lamp mean that all was well?

Rewrite each sentence correctly.

17 helga would prefer to go to gorm

18 the chapters title is seeking the magus

Answers and explanations on pages 119–120

TEXTS IN CONTEXT

Text 2

Book review

Title: *The Extremely Inconvenient Adventures of Bronte Mettlestone*

Author: Jaclyn Moriarty

Summary of plot: This story is told by the protagonist Bronte Mettlestone, now aged twelve. Bronte recounts events in her life that occurred when she was ten and she found out that her parents had been murdered by pirates. They left a will, in which there are specific instructions for Bronte to follow and the threat of terrible consequences if she doesn't. The instructions take Bronte on her 'inconvenient adventures'.

Writing style: The author uses tongue-in-cheek humour and word play. For example, Bronte first hears of her parents' deaths when a letter arrives to state they have been 'taken out' by pirates. Bronte doesn't realise this is bad news as she'd been 'taken out' to afternoon tea quite often and had enjoyed it. Another example of word play is when the parents' will is discussed in light of three kinds of 'will'. As well as the will which describes what the deceased wished to be done after their deaths, the dog's name is Will (only with a capital 'W') and Bronte admits to having a strong will.

Setting and character development: The characters are varied and entertaining, with pirates, fairies, water sprites and dragons in fantastical settings.

Recommendation: I think children aged nine and over will enjoy this story. It has great characters, magic and spells, and mysteries to solve. It is told with humour but it is also about families and relationships. You'll like this book if you liked Lemony Snicket's *A Series of Unfortunate Events*.

Reviewed by Holly Banister, age 12

1 Fantasy stories often have quests or missions. What is the quest or mission for Text 1 in Unit 19A?

....

2 The purpose of Text 2 is to

- **A** convince adults to buy the book for their children.
- **B** summarise the plot of a story.
- **C** give an opinion about a story.
- **D** persuade children over nine to read a story.

3 What is a protagonist? ....

....

4 Bronte's parents had been 'taken out' by pirates. Taken out is a euphemism for

- **A** kidnapped.
- **B** entertained.
- **C** killed.
- **D** beaten up.

5 Find and write evidence from Text 1 in Unit 19A that indicates it is a fantasy story.

....

....

6 Find and write evidence from Text 2 that indicates *The Extremely Inconvenient Adventures of Bronte Mettlestone* is a fantasy story.

....

....

Get creative

7 Write a fantasy story.

Answers and explanations on page 120

READING AND COMPREHENSION

Text 1

Safari

From: Nana Jo and Gpa Ted <joandted@gmail.com>
Today 3.41 pm

Dear Matilda

We are writing from Botswana in Africa. It's so exciting. We love our tour so far. English is the country's official language so that makes it easy for us to communicate. The local language is called Setswana. Three-quarters of the country is covered by the Kalahari Desert and within the desert's borders is the Okavango Delta, which is one of the seven natural wonders of Africa and a UNESCO World Heritage site. It is a wetland when the floodwaters flow in from the central African highlands, 1000 km away. The wetland attracts migrating herds of animals such as magnificent elephants and zebra.

The philosophy of the ecotourism company we're using is to look after the local people so that they see value in tourism and therefore have a vested interest in saving the animals and their habitats. It would be a tragedy to lose any of the animal species. The company funds education, health and agriculture activities in the local community. The local people are employed in conservation efforts and they are trained in trades such as building and electrical, or they are given traineeships in wildlife conservation. The company has also purchased land to increase the migration corridor for wild animals. It's a really good thing. You'd love it.

We even saw some very old rock paintings by the indigenous hunter-gatherer people, the San. There's evidence in rock paintings that they have lived here for tens of thousands of years. It's amazing to see something that's so old.

We hope everyone at home in Oz is well. We'll give you a call when we get back. We miss you. Love to Mum.

Love Nana and G'pa XOXOXO

1 Matilda lives in ....

2 The Okavango Delta is a wetland inside a ....

3 Ecotourism means

- **A** when tourists pay to save wild animals.
- **B** tourism which uses wild animals.
- **C** environmentally sustainable tourism.
- **D** tourism which focuses on herds of wild elephants.

4 What can you infer about the reason the company wanted to increase the migration corridor?

....

....

5 Why is it important for local communities to value tourism?

....

....

....

....

6 What judgements can you make about the way Nana and G'pa correspond with Matilda?

....

....

....

Answers and explanations on page 120

SPELLING

Rewrite the misspelt words in questions 1–3.

1 The philosify is to look after the local people.

2 The area is called the Kalahari Dessert.

3 The delta's waters flow in from the hilands.

4 Add a prefix to this word from the text: **valued**. Then write a definition for the new word.

5 Write three words from the word family that includes **communicate**.

VOCABULARY

6 Use a dictionary that includes word origins. Explain the origin and meaning of this word from the text: **indigenous**.

7 Circle the word that has the nearest meaning to the underlined word.

The wetland attracts migrating animals.

A drifting B journeying
C walking D flying

8 Choose the correct definition for this word from the text: **tragedy**.

A bad luck
B an unfortunate event
C when people are forced off their land
D a disastrous event

9 Use a dictionary. Write a definition for this phrase from the text: **official language**.

Circle the word that does **not** belong.

10 A evidence B proof
C signs D marks

11 A beliefs B actions
C philosophy D values

GRAMMAR

12 Which pronoun correctly completes the sentence?

The San have been forced off their ancestral land. We'd like to help ....

A they B us C them D those

13 Rewrite this sentence in the present tense.

The company funded the two housing projects.

14 Circle the adverbial clause.

We will give you a call when we get back.

15 Choose the best connective to complete the sentence.

The internet is poor here (furthermore / however / therefore / nevertheless) we haven't sent many emails..

PUNCTUATION

16 Circle the sentence that is punctuated correctly.

A The Okavango Delta is a UNESCO world heritage site.
B There are rock paintings that are thousand's of years old.
C We'll give you a call as soon as we can.

Rewrite each sentence correctly.

17 unesco does a good job said ted

18 were enjoying the tour of botswana said nana

Answers and explanations on page 120

TEXTS IN CONTEXT

Text 2

New

Reply

Reply all

Forward

Delete

Archive
Undo

Dear Nana and G'pa

Your trip sounds amazing. I would love to go to Africa one day and see zebras and elephants. I love the photos you've posted online. The range of animals in the Okavango Delta looks amazing. I looked up the Delta. It's a UNESCO World Heritage–listed site. The Great Barrier Reef is listed as one too. That's a big contrast to the Kalahari Desert but it has a great range of animals too—all of them underwater, of course.

I like the fact that you call yourselves ecotourists. Mum says we are ecotourists too whenever we travel. We like to experience nature without harming any aspect of the environment. She says, 'We love visiting natural places so we have to be mindful of our behaviour so we don't destroy that which we love.' She'd love to visit Antarctica but worries that too many tourists go there already and it's going to be ruined. I don't agree with her because I think that all the governments in charge of Antarctica would not let that happen. I want to go to Antarctica. Perhaps I could work on a research vessel when I'm old enough.

Rock art in Kakadu National Park

Mum and I are saving up to go to Kakadu. Mum says that's the number one ecotourism destination in Australia and guess what? It's World Heritage listed too. People love it because of its beauty and cultural significance. Did you know there are more than 5000 rock-art sites in Kakadu? People have lived there for 65 000 years. That's amazing!

Maybe you can come to Kakadu with us and then you'll have seen rock art in Africa and Australia. I wonder which rock art is older.

Enjoy the rest of your trip.

Love you and miss you too, Matilda XxxxxxXxxxxxX

1 Choose **all** that apply. The purpose of both Text 1 in Unit 20A and Text 2 is to
- A describe a tour.
- B inform about Botswana.
- C communicate with a loved one.
- D present a point of view.

2 Which of the following apply to Text 2?
- A informal language
- B conversational tone
- C terminology specific to the topics
- D formal language

3 The main subject of Text 2 is
- A the importance of tourism.
- B amazing natural places to visit.
- C places where Matilda has been.
- D Matilda's grandparents' holiday.

4 G'pa likely stands for
- A Granddad.
- B Grandpa.
- C Great pa.
- D Grandfather.

5 Choose **all** that apply. You can judge that every member of Matilda's family is interested in
- A conservation.
- B travel.
- C the environment.
- D human rights issues such as health and education.

6 Make a judgement. How is Matilda's family similar to and different from your own?

....

....

Get creative

7 Find out about one of the great migrations in Africa. Write a report.

Answers and explanations on page 120

 **Text 1**

Ivory

One hundred years ago there were 10 million elephants. Now there are around 40 000 Asian elephants and 400 000 African elephants left in the world. Elephants, killed for their ivory, have their tusks and faces hacked off, sometimes while they are still alive. Their carcasses are left to rot; their babies orphaned.

Rangers are employed to protect them but the elephants range across vast areas of countryside and poachers, usually poor locals funded by criminal gangs, use drones and other high-tech equipment to track them and avoid rangers. It's a constant battle for rangers to stay ahead of poachers.

Countries such as the UK, the USA, France, Belgium, China and Kenya have destroyed their stockpiles of confiscated ivory. Governments choose to destroy ivory to prove that it has no market value. It is hoped that this will discourage poachers from killing elephants and stop dealers from buying or selling ivory. Ivory's only value should be on a living elephant.

People who buy ivory view it as a luxury item and a status symbol. Most poached ivory is sold on Asian black markets. The Chinese Government declared ivory trade illegal from 1 January 2018. Some airports in Africa use ivory sniffer dogs on routes to China, Vietnam and Laos.

Conservation organisations want governments of countries where there is still trade in ivory to improve law enforcement and hand out harsher penalties to poachers or people caught dealing in ivory.

1 Find and write **two** facts that make it difficult for rangers to stop the ivory trade.

....

....

....

....

2 What do some countries do with confiscated ivory?

....

....

3 Choose **all** that apply. Which of the following would be ways to 'improve law enforcement' (lines 18–19)?

- **A** arresting people who have ivory products
- **B** putting poachers in jail for a long time
- **C** arresting rangers for tracking elephants
- **D** jailing or fining people who make money from ivory
- **E** arresting people who buy or sell ivory
- **F** catching and punishing people connected with ivory poaching

4 Choose **all** that apply. Which statements can be inferred from the text?

- **A** People buy ivory jewellery from poachers.
- **B** A black market is used for selling legal goods.
- **C** Ivory sells for a high price.
- **D** There are places around the world where people can buy ivory.
- **E** Rangers and poachers try to outsmart each other.
- **F** Elephants are in danger of extinction.

5 Why would local people become poachers? Choose **all** that apply.

- **A** They enjoy hunting.
- **B** They need money.
- **C** They love to wear ivory.
- **D** They need jobs.
- **E** They are skilled at finding elephants.

6 People want to own ivory to show

- **A** they don't need to obey laws.
- **B** how rich they are.
- **C** they value elephants.
- **D** they do not care about conservation.

Answers and explanations on page 121

SPELLING

Rewrite the misspelt words in questions 1–3.

1 The rhinoserus has ivory.

2 The hippopotimus has ivory.

3 Babies are orphined.

4 Add a prefix to this word from the text: **protected**. Then write a definition for the new word.

5 Write three words from the word family that includes **destroy**.

VOCABULARY

6 Use a dictionary that includes word origins. Explain the origin and meaning of this word from the text: **confiscated**.

7 Circle the answer that has the nearest meaning to the underlined word.

Stockpiles have been destroyed.

A items for sale B accumulated goods
C stock in a pile D a thief's hoard

8 Choose the correct definition for **carcasses** in the text.

A herds B skeletons
C bodies D stomachs

9 Use a dictionary. Write a definition for this word from the text: **ranger**.

Circle the word that does **not** belong.

10 A mild B stern
C severe D harsh

11 A massacre B butchery
C death D bloodbath

GRAMMAR

12 Which pronoun completes the sentence correctly?

Body parts are sold to healers. Healers use .... because they believe they have magic powers.

A it B they C them D he

13 Rewrite this sentence in the present tense.

Elephants were killed by poachers.

14 Circle the adverbial clause.

The ranger arrived after we'd pitched the tent.

15 Choose the best connective to complete the sentence.

Ivory poaching is cruel and (alternatively / consequently / meanwhile / nevertheless) it must be stopped.

PUNCTUATION

16 Circle the sentence that is punctuated correctly.

A It's a constant battle for rangers.
B It's ivory was hacked off.
C Poachers' hacked off the tusks.

Rewrite each sentence correctly.

17 babies witnessed their mothers deaths

18 if people understood poaching they wouldnt buy ivory

Answers and explanations on page 121

TEXTS IN CONTEXT

Text 2

How to save elephants

1 Educate local communities to value elephants and want to protect them.
2 Educate people around the world not to buy ivory.
3 Improve elephant protection using the latest technology (drones, collared trackers).
4 Educate people worldwide about the decline in elephant numbers, how baby elephants are orphaned when their mothers are killed and about the trauma for the babies who witness their mothers' deaths. Make people who own ivory feel ashamed.
5 Protect habitats. Buy Certified Fair Trade coffee and Forest Stewardship Council timber to ensure elephant habitats are not destroyed. Do not buy any products that contain palm oil. (Palm oil plantations replace forest habitats.)
6 Support the work of conservation organisations. (Hold community or school fundraising events.) Write letters and petitions asking for increased law enforcement in countries where elephants need protection. Demand severe penalties for all wildlife crimes.

Note: There is an international agreement between governments that is meant to protect species from extinction, e.g. by prohibiting ivory trade. This is the Convention on International Trade in Endangered Species of Wild Fauna and Flora (CITES). There are more than 180 member countries, including Australia.

Vulture massacre

Mozambique, February 2018

Eighty-seven critically endangered vultures died after consuming poison that had been planted in the carcasses of poached elephants. Poachers often kill vultures because they circle in the sky over carcasses and alert rangers to the poachers' presence. The bodies of these vultures had been mutilated and their body parts taken for traditional medicines used by healers in Sub-Saharan Africa where some people believe that vultures have magical powers.

In Africa all adult elephants have tusks. In Asia only some male elephants have tusks. Ivory also grows on the rhinoceros, walrus, hippopotamus and narwhal.

1 What does 'CITES' stand for? 

2 For which **two** reasons are vultures killed?

....

....

3 For which purposes were Text 1 in Unit 21A and Text 2 written? Circle **two** answers for each text.

Text 1: **A** recount **B** entertain
C inform **D** explain
E persuade **F** describe

Text 2: **A** recount **B** entertain
C inform **D** explain
E persuade **F** describe

4 CITES is 'meant to protect species from extinction'. What does 'meant' tell readers?

....

....

5 What is the aim of Point 4?

....

....

....

6 What evidence tells readers that local communities need education about vultures?

....

....

....

....

Get creative

7 Do some research about an endangered species under threat due to wildlife crime. Report your findings.

Answers and explanations on page 121

READING AND COMPREHENSION

Text 1

All that glitters is not gold

NOTE: This is a rap poem.

No Chris'mas gifts for us this year
Instead we're going to volunteer
to do some good for those in need
and those who have no families.
We'll be nice to one another
we'll help each other
and not cause bother.
(A change, Mum says,
from squabbling all day
and getting sent outside to play.)
Last year I got my Christmas gifts
but one week later began a new list.
Satisfaction was fleeting.
Always wanting
the next thing.
Greed is bad for Planet E.
Satisfaction's tempor'ry.
Too much greed and wastage all round.
People starving—
barren ground.
Trees cut down for no good cause.
Rubbish piling mound on mound.
Plastic in the ocean?
What? No way!
People have to stop or pay.
People have to feel and see
that climate change is not free;
soon there'll be no Planet E.
This year we're giving
not receiving—
donating things
that we don't need.
No Christmas tree.
No decorations,
plastic forks or plastic plates.
So much waste—
It's outrageous!
All that glitters is not gold.
Festive season's glitter gets old.
(Gone to landfill so I'm told.)
We're not buying
what shouldn't be sold.
Living lighter—that's our goal.
Helping Earth and helping others—
Taking on a whole new role.

1 What usually happens in the narrator's house on Christmas Day?

....

....

2 The narrator complains about things that are wrong with the world. List them.

3 The words 'but one week later began a new list' (line 14) implies a list of
- A unwanted gifts.
- B things to donate.
- C ways family members can help each other.
- D wanted gifts.

4 What do people have to 'feel and see' (line 28)?
- A feel sad and see what they can do
- B feel angry and see the plastic in the ocean
- C feel sorry for the earth and where their rubbish goes
- D feel responsible and see what's happening to the earth

5 'All that glitters is not gold' means
- A think about the true impact of your choices.
- B just because it looks good does not mean it is good.
- C gold glitters and is precious but gold mining destroys nature.
- D gold might seem good but look closer and it is not.

6 Choose **all** that apply. How might 'ground' become 'barren' (line 22)?
- A agricultural overuse
- B climate change
- C pollution
- D lack of rain
- E Native animals have eaten all the vegetation.
- F Nature is out of balance.

Answers and explanations on page 121

SPELLING

Rewrite the misspelt words in questions 1–3.

1 giving not recieving

2 Families squabling all day

3 It's outragous!

4 Add a prefix to this word from the text: **satisfaction.** Then write a definition for the new word.

5 Write three words from the word family that includes **volunteer**.

VOCABULARY

6 Use a dictionary that includes word origins. Explain the origin and meaning of this word from the text: **Christmas**.

7 Circle the answer that has the nearest meaning to the underlined word.

Satisfaction's <u>tempor'ry</u>.

A short-lived B long-lasting
C worth it D tempting

8 Choose the correct definition for this word from the text: **donating**.

A offering money to charities
B giving C helping
D giving second-hand things to others

9 Use a dictionary. Write a definition for this phrase from the text: **festive season**.

Circle the word or phrase that does **not** belong.

10 A temporary B permanent
C fleeting D transient

11 A sparkle B decorate
C glitter D shine

GRAMMAR

12 Which pronoun completes the sentence correctly?

No Chris'mas gifts for .... this year. Instead we're going to volunteer.

A they B we C us D them

13 Rewrite this sentence in the present tense.

Those in need will be helped by the family.

14 Circle the adverbial clause.

While I used to love decorations, I don't love them anymore.

15 Rewrite the sentence, adding the dependent (subordinate) clause: who volunteers for Landcare

My mum gives her time to help the environment.

PUNCTUATION

16 Circle the sentence that is punctuated correctly.

A Id just want the next thing.
B Where going to volunteer.
C We're not buying what shouldn't be sold.

Rewrite each sentence correctly.

17 were giving things that we dont need

18 wwf stands for world wildlife fund

Answers and explanations on page 121

TEXTS IN CONTEXT

Text 2

Volunteering

BECOME A VOLUNTEER

Be part of something that makes a difference to people, animals or the environment.

- Help other children or aged-care residents: collect tinned food for people who do not have enough to eat; visit elderly people to read or talk to them; organise fundraising events.
- Help the environment: collect rubbish, plant trees, clear weeds.
- Persuade your family or school to support a particular charity or campaign: save gorillas, save whales, save koalas, provide safe water for people who have no running water, help refugees, help people with disabilities or children living with cancer.
- There are many organisations in Australia where young people can volunteer.

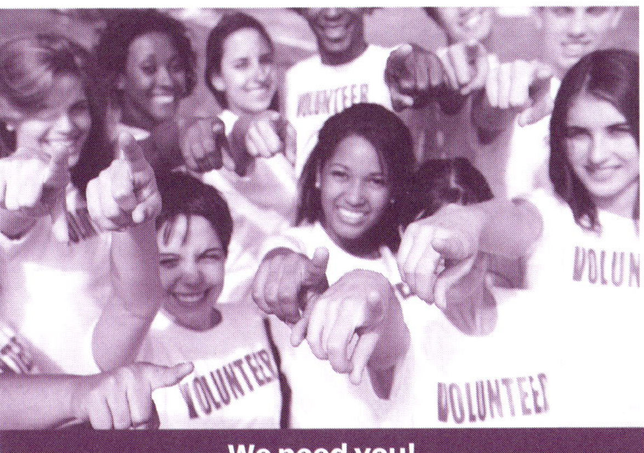

We need you!

GET INVOLVED. Feel good about yourself.

Join the millions of Australians who volunteer. Search for 'volunteering in Australia'. NOW.

(NB For many groups and organisations you will need to join with a parent or adult family member.)

1 Text 2 says that volunteering makes you feel good about
- A others.
- B animals.
- C the environment.
- D yourself.

2 'NB' (line 21) is used in Text 2. It stands for a Latin phrase, *nota bene*. What do you think it means?
- A make notes
- B notice this
- C note well
- D not of benefit

3 What 'shouldn't be sold' (line 44) according to Text 1 in Unit 22A?

....

....

4 In Text 1 in Unit 22A who makes choices about what should and shouldn't be sold?

....

....

....

5 In Text 1 (Unit 22A) what does 'Living lighter' (line 45) mean?
- A that the earth pays when people do irresponsible things
- B people have to stop or pay
- C not creating so much waste or using so many resources
- D that the cost of climate change will destroy earth

6 How are Text 1 in Unit 22A and Text 2 similar?
- A Both are about volunteering to do good things.
- B Both aim to persuade people to do something good.
- C Both have a theme of caring for others or for the planet.
- D The narrator in Text 1 intends to volunteer.

7 Write a rap poem about a cause or interest that you feel strongly about.

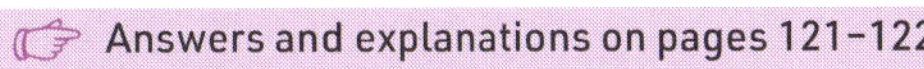
Answers and explanations on pages 121–122

Text 1

Elite athletes

1 Some governments around the world subsidise their elite athletes so that they can compete internationally. Governments do this mostly for reasons of national pride since nations compete against each other, but also to inspire ordinary citizens to play sport and get fitter and healthier.

2 Governments subsidise sporting teams or sporting organisations, provide grants, build stadiums, provide equipment, and so on. Most athletes need jobs to support themselves or they need to find sponsors and products to endorse. Clothing, food, sporting equipment, sports nutrition, vitamin supplements, watches and vehicles are the typical products that athletes can promote through endorsement deals. Usually only the top athletes or the most well-known ones can secure sponsors or endorsements.

3 Athletes can also potentially win prize money in competitions but the top athletes in the world earn more money through endorsements than they do through prize money. Some athletes become very wealthy. Other athletes need the financial support of family members or sympathetic employers for the hours it takes to train and the time away from employment that it takes to compete.

4 Some countries' governments have no money at all to spare for athletes. The money in those countries must be used for housing, education, hospitals, roads and other essentials for everyday citizens. Athletes in those countries find their own ways to fund their sporting passions.

5 There is an argument in Australia that the money spent by the government on elite athletes and sports, and on sending athletes to international events such as the Olympics, Paralympics and Commonwealth Games, would be better spent on programs that get everyday Australians fitter and healthier. Some people argue that the benefits to Australia in funding elite sports are outweighed by the costs.

1 Why might a government pay for sports?

....

....

2 Choose **all** that apply. When a government funds sports, what other areas might get less money?

A housing **B** education
C hospitals **D** roads

3 What is national pride?

A being proud of your country's athletes
B when you compete against other countries
C being proud when you win a sporting contest
D being proud of your country

4 What does the term 'elite athletes' imply?

A only athletes that win gold medals
B only the most popular athletes
C only the best athletes
D only the athletes people watch on television

5 How do athletes get money? List **six** ways.

....

....

....

....

....

....

6 Summarise paragraph 5. Some people think that government funding for elite athletes

A is money well spent.
B is a total waste.
C could be put to better use elsewhere.
D is justified.

Answers and explanations on page 122

SPELLING

Rewrite the misspelt words in questions 1–3.

1 Governments can subsadise sports.

2 We watch the Paralimpics.

3 Benefits are outwayed by costs.

4 Add a prefix to this word from the text: **national**. Then write a definition for the new word.

5 Write three words from the word family that includes **subsidise**.

VOCABULARY

6 Use a dictionary that includes word origins. Explain the origin and meaning of this word from the text: **Olympics**.

7 Circle the answer that has the nearest meaning to the underlined word.

Governments can provide <u>grants</u> to athletes.

A gifts
B weekly payments
C money that needs to be repaid eventually
D money that does not need to be repaid

8 Choose the correct definition for this word from the text: **supplement**.

A medicine
B vitamin tablets
C something to improve your health
D tablets taken in addition to food

9 Use a dictionary. Write a definition for this word from the text: **endorsement**.

Circle the word that does **not** belong.

10 A sympathetic B unkind
C compassionate D understanding

11 A reject B endorse
C approve D recommend

GRAMMAR

12 Which pronoun completes the sentence correctly?

Most athletes need jobs to support ....

A him B themselves
C ourselves D us

13 Rewrite this sentence in the present tense.

Prize money can be won by athletes.

14 Circle the adverbial clause.

Whenever I watch the Paralympics I feel proud.

15 Choose the best connective to complete the sentence.

(Conversely / Subsequently / Thereafter / Whenever) I watch the Paralympics I feel proud.

PUNCTUATION

16 Circle the sentence that is punctuated correctly.

A We watch the Olympic and Paralympic games.
B The 2018 Commonwealth Games' were held on the Gold Coast.
C Some countries' governments have no money for athletes.

Rewrite each sentence correctly.

17 clothing food watches and vehicles are products that athletes endorse

18 the governments grants to athletes are being questioned

Answers and explanations on page 122

Text 2

Top athletes use

NutriBLAZE

"I use NutriBLAZE for energy and stamina. It makes me more competitive."

"I recommend NutriBLAZE. I love the results."

"I take NutriBLAZE every day. It makes me a winner."

"I could not compete without NutriBLAZE."

FEEL BETTER LOOK BETTER DO BETTER

GO FOR IT!

✓Enhanced performance ✓Increased energy levels
✓Increased endurance ✓Sharper brain function

NutriBLAZE: It works!

1 What is the main slogan for NutriBLAZE?
- A Top athletes use NutriBLAZE.
- B Look better
- C Feel better
- D Do better
- E Go for it!

2 Choose **all** that apply. The logo for NutriBLAZE includes a lightning bolt to symbolise
- A a burst of energy.
- B self-destruction.
- C speed.
- D power.
- E danger.
- F rain.
- G thunder.

3 Choose **all** that apply. A brand chooses particular athletes to endorse their products because they seem to be
- A healthy.
- B fit.
- C attractive.
- D famous.
- E unknown.
- F popular.
- G ordinary.
- H trustworthy.
- I likeable.
- J experts in the product.
- K winners.
- L idolised.
- M people's heroes.

4 If an athlete endorsed a health brand and was then found to have been a drug cheat, what might the public think?

....

....

....

5 How are Text 1 in Unit 23A and Text 2 related?

....

....

....

6 Why is it that only top athletes get endorsement deals?

....

....

....

....

7 Design an advertisement that uses endorsements.

Answers and explanations on page 122

 Text 1

Grandfather's Chair

GRANDFATHER had been sitting in his old arm-chair all that pleasant afternoon, while the children were pursuing their various sports far off or near at hand, Sometimes you would have said, 'Grandfather is asleep;' but still, even when his eyes were closed, his thoughts were with the young people. …

He heard the voice of Laurence, who had taken possession of a heap of decayed branches which the gardener had lopped from the fruit-trees, and was building a little hut for his cousin Clara and himself. He heard Clara's gladsome voice, too, as she weeded and watered the flower-bed. …

He could have counted every footstep that Charley took, as he trundled his wheelbarrow along the gravel-walk. And though' Grandfather was old and gray-haired, yet his heart leaped with joy whenever little Alice came fluttering, like a butterfly, into the room. …

At last the children grew weary of their sports, … So they came into the room together, and clustered round Grandfather's great chair. Little Alice … climbed his knee. …

'Grandfather,' said little Alice … 'I am very tired now. You must tell me a story to make me go to sleep.'

'That is not what story-tellers like,' answered Grandfather, smiling. 'They are better satisfied when they can keep their auditors awake.'

'But here are Laurence, and Charley, and I,' cried cousin Clara, who was twice as old as little Alice. 'We will all three keep wide awake. And pray, Grandfather, tell us a story about this strange-looking old chair.'

Now, the chair in which Grandfather sat was made of oak, which had grown dark with age, but had been rubbed and polished till it shone as bright as mahogany. It was very large and heavy, and had a back that rose high above Grandfather's white head. This back was curiously carved … to represent flowers, and foliage … On the very tip-top of the chair, over the head of Grandfather himself, was a likeness of a lion's head, which had such a savage grin that you would almost expect to hear it growl and snarl.'

(Excerpt from 'The Whole History of Grandfather's Chair' by Nathaniel Hawthorne, *True Stories from New England History,* 1840)

 Text 2

My grandmother

My grandmother is 66, which is pretty young compared with other grandmothers of children in my class.

My grandmother lives with us. Mum is divorced and Nan is a widow so we three live together. It's pretty cool because Nan is usually on my side in any family dispute (I can count on her to stick up for me if she thinks Mum is being too strict) and she is a better cook than my mum so I am doubly lucky.

Nan works part-time as a medical receptionist. She used to be a theatre nurse but that job got too hard as she got older. Nan tells me to work hard at school and not to muck up in class and risk my education. She thinks I'd make a great nurse or doctor because I am compassionate. I think I'd rather be an architect but we'll see. She says I won't disappoint her whatever I choose.

1 In Text 1 Grandfather had been
A snoozing.
B dreaming of the children.
C daydreaming about the children.
D alert to the children's whereabouts.

2 'the children were pursuing their various sports' (lines 2–3, Text 1)

This means the children were
A engaged in different energetic activities.
B playing different sports in the garden.
C playing a game together.
D learning various sports.

3 In Text 1 why is Clara so interested in the chair?
A It is large and heavy with interesting carvings of foliage, fruit and a snarling lion's head.
B She is not allowed to sit on it so it must be magical.
C It is obviously Grandfather's special chair as it is mentioned in the title.
D Grandfather won't tell where he got it so Clara thinks there is a secret to uncover.

4 In Text 1 what do the children want Grandfather to do?
A Come and play in the garden with them.
B Tell them a bedtime story.
C Go back to sleep.
D Tell them the story of the chair.

5 Make a judgement about the grandfather in Text 1.
A He is loving and kindly.
B He is forgetful.
C He is lazy.
D He spends a lot of time sleeping.

6 Choose **all** that apply. Make judgements about the relationship between the children and grandfather in Text 1.
A He is stern and polices their activities.
B He watches them constantly to keep them safe.
C He is aware of their safety without being overly protective.
D He is generous with his time.
E The children give him great joy.
F The children pester and annoy him.
G He allows the children to boss him and bully him.
H He'd rather not be bothered with the activities or the children.

7 In Text 1 how is Alice confused about the purpose of a story and what is she told by Grandfather?

....

....

....

8 Circle the correct answers in the brackets to complete the sentence.

Text 1 is told in the (first / second / third) person and Text 2 is told in the (first / second / third) person.

9 In Text 2 Nan is
A loving and caring.
B strict but fair.
C too soft on the writer.
D too busy to be very involved in the writer's life.

10 Choose **all** that apply. In Text 2 Nan values
A education.
B arguments for the sake of arguments.
C hard work.
D teaching her grandson how to cook.
E family.

11 Find and write **two** emotive phrases used in Text 1.

....

....

12 What two things will likely happen next in Text 1?

....

....

Answers and explanations on page 122

The incorrect word in each sentence has been circled. Write the correct spelling of each word.

1 It was a (plesant) afternoon.

2 The children were building with (decayd) branches.

3 The chair was (curiesly) carved.

4 (Folige) was carved at the top.

5 Charley (trundeld) his wheelbarrow.

6 The carving was a (likness) of a lion's head.

7 Choose the correct answer to complete the sentence.

Clara's voice could be heard as .... weeded and watered the flower-bed.

A they **B** them **C** her **D** she

8 In which sentence is **frown** used as a verb?

A His frown indicated his displeasure.
B Grandpa had a perpetual frown.
C They frown on unruly behaviour in the museum.
D Her frown lines were very prominent.

9 Which answer completes the sentence correctly?

The children .... played in the garden all afternoon.

A had **B** had been
C were **D** was

10 Circle the subject of the sentence.

The chair was carved from oak.

11 Circle the verb or verb group in the sentence.

Nan had been a theatre nurse.

12 Which sentence shows the present tense?

A The children often enjoyed stories.
B The children enjoyed stories.
C The children enjoy stories.
D The children usually enjoyed stories.

13 Which adverbial completes the sentence correctly?

Grandpa's thoughts were ....

A with the young people
B over the young people
C beyond the young people
D until the young people

14 Underline the dependent clause in the sentence.

On the top of the chair was a lion's head, which had a savage grin.

15 Which sentence uses quotation marks correctly?

A 'Tell us a story,' begged Alice.'
B 'I can tell you a story to keep you awake, said Grandfather.'
C 'I am sleepy,' said Alice.
D 'Grandfather said,' Hop up here.

16 Which sentence is punctuated correctly?

A Laurence, Charley, Alice, and Clara wanted to hear a story.
B Grandfather's hair was grey.
C 'Its such a big old chair,' said Clara.
D Nathaniel Hawthorne, is the author.

Answers and explanations on page 122

Text 1

The Wind in the Willows by Kenneth Grahame

(1908, Charles Scribner's Sons)

'Toad,' she said presently, 'Just listen, please. I have an aunt who is a washerwoman.'

'There, there,' said Toad, graciously and affably, 'never mind; think no more about it. I have several aunts who ought to be washerwomen.'

'Do be quiet a minute, Toad,' said the girl. 'You talk too much, that's your chief fault, and I'm trying to think, and you hurt my head. As I said, I have an aunt who is a washerwoman; she does the washing for all the prisoners in this castle—we try to keep any paying business of that sort in the family, you understand. Now, this is what occurs to me: you're very rich—at least you're always telling me so—and she's very poor. A few pounds wouldn't make any difference to you, and it would mean a lot to her. Now, I think if she were properly approached—squared, I believe is the word you animals use—you could come to some arrangement by which she would let you have her dress and bonnet and so on, and you could escape from the castle as the official washerwoman. You're very alike in many respects—particularly about the figure.'

'We're not,' said the Toad in a huff. 'I have a very elegant figure—for what I am.'

'So has my aunt,' replied the girl, 'for what she is. But have it your own way. You horrid, proud, ungrateful animal, when I'm sorry for you, and trying to help you!'

'Yes, yes, that's all right; thank you very much indeed,' said the Toad hurriedly. 'But look here! you wouldn't surely have Mr. Toad, of Toad Hall, going about the country disguised as a washerwoman!'

'Then you can stop here as a Toad,' replied the girl with much spirit. 'I suppose you want to go off in a coach-and-four!'

1 Name the characters who would likely appear in the next scene of the story.

....

....

2 Describe the setting for the extract.

....

....

3 What is Toad's predicament?

....

....

4 What obstacles are there to solving Toad's predicament?

....

....

5 Which words describe Toad's character? Choose **all** that apply.

- **A** vain
- **B** proud
- **C** hardworking
- **D** prejudiced
- **E** pompous
- **F** thoughtful
- **G** respectful
- **H** easy to talk to
- **I** boastful

6 What does Toad think when the girl first tells him her aunt is a washerwoman?

....

....

....

....

Answers and explanations on pages 122–123

SPELLING

Rewrite the misspelt words in questions 1–3.

1 We could come to some arrangment.

2 You can escape from the castle as the offishil washerwoman.

3 You are an ungratful animal.

4 Add a prefix to this word from the text: **difference**. Then write a definition for the new word.

5 Write three words from the word family that includes **escaped**.

VOCABULARY

6 Use a dictionary that includes word origins. Explain the origin and meaning of this word from the text: **coach**.

7 Circle the answer that has the nearest meaning to the underlined word.

'There, there' Toad replied affably.

A in a friendly way
B in a cranky way
C in a superior way
D in a boastful way

8 Choose the correct definition for this word from the text: **squared**.

A politely B pleadingly
C fairly D strongly

9 Use a dictionary. Write a definition for this word group from the text: **the figure**.

Circle the word that does **not** belong.

10 A graciously B courteously
C churlishly D civilly

11 A stylish B uncultured
C elegant D tasteful

GRAMMAR

12 Circle the extended noun group that includes an adjectival clause.

I have an aunt who is a washerwoman.

13 Circle the modal verb that expresses the least certainty.

You (may / can / might) read for ten more minutes then it's bedtime.

14 Add a modal adverb that expresses certainty.

I could .... become a lawyer.

15 Add a connective to complete the sentence.

.... a few pounds wouldn't make any difference to you, it would mean a lot to her.

PUNCTUATION

16 Which sentence is punctuated correctly?

A Unfortunately, Ian made rock hard scones.
B Unfortunately, Ian made rock-hard scones.
C Unfortunately, Ian made rock, hard scones.

Rewrite each sentence correctly.

17 youll need to be quiet said the girl

18 the girl said dont be so annoying

Answers and explanations on page 123

TEXTS IN CONTEXT

Text 2

The Secret Garden by Frances Hodgson Burnett

(1911, William Heinemann)

So long as Mistress Mary's mind was full of disagreeable thoughts about her dislikes and sour opinions of people and her determination not to be pleased by or interested in anything, she was a yellow-faced, sickly, bored and wretched child. Circumstances, however, were very kind to her, though she was not at all aware of it. They began to push her about for her own good. When her mind gradually filled itself with robins, and moorland cottages crowded with children, with queer crabbed old gardeners and common little Yorkshire housemaids, with springtime and with secret gardens coming alive day by day, and also with a moor boy and his 'creatures,' there was no room left for the disagreeable thoughts which affected her liver and her digestion and made her yellow and tired.

So long as Colin shut himself up in his room and thought only of his fears and weakness and his detestation of people who looked at him and reflected hourly on humps and early death, he was a hysterical half-crazy little hypochondriac who knew nothing of the sunshine and the spring and also did not know that he could get well and could stand upon his feet if he tried to do it. When new beautiful thoughts began to push out the old hideous ones, life began to come back to him, his blood ran healthily through his veins and strength poured into him like a flood. His scientific experiment was quite practical and simple and there was nothing weird about it at all. Much more surprising things can happen to anyone who, when a disagreeable or discouraged thought comes into his mind, just has the sense to remember in time and push it out by putting in an agreeable determinedly courageous one. Two things cannot be in one place.

'Where you tend a rose, my lad, a thistle cannot grow.'

1. As well as to entertain, what likely purpose might the novels in both Text 1 (Unit 24A) and Text 2 share?

2. Choose **either** Text 1 in Unit 24A **or** Text 2 and describe the intended reader of the text at the time it was written.

3. Write four words or phrases that establish the setting of Text 2 as **not** modern day.

4. Compare the children. How are they different?

5. *'Where you tend a rose, my lad, a thistle cannot grow.'* What is the meaning of this statement in line 20?

6. If you had to choose either *The Secret Garden* or *The Wind in the Willows* to read, which would you choose and why?

7. Find and read a novel published around 1900 and write a brief review.

Answers and explanations on page 123

READING AND COMPREHENSION

Text 1

Charlie Perkins and the Freedom Ride

In 1965 a group of students from Sydney University formed SAFA (Student Action for Aborigines). The group elected Indigenous Australian student Charles Perkins as President. Inspired by events in America that highlighted racial discrimination there, SAFA's goal was to investigate and report on the treatment of First Nations Australians in country NSW to the wider Australian community and internationally.

The group hired a bus and set out from Sydney, visiting places such as Dubbo, Walgett, Moree, Tenterfield, Grafton, Lismore and Kempsey, to survey the living conditions of First Nations Peoples. They were referred to as the Freedom Riders and they discovered evidence of racial discrimination in many country towns. In Moree, for example, they found that the Segregationist Statute of 1955 was enforced so First Australians were not allowed entry to the public swimming pool. When the university protesters tried to get First Nations children into the pool there was a violent altercation with some townspeople wanting to uphold the Segregationist Statute. The Freedom Riders were spat on and pelted with rotten fruit and vegetables. Violence escalated until finally the Mayor of Moree intervened to rescind the Statute and allow Indigenous people to use the pool.

The Freedom Ride drew attention to racial discrimination in Australia. A referendum in 1967 was supported by 90% of Australians. It approved the inclusion of First Australians in the census so that they would be counted in the population for purposes of federal funding to the states. The referendum also gave the Federal Government power to make laws specifically for First Nations people. This took away the states' powers, which varied greatly across Australia.

A used Australian postage stamp from 2013 showing Charles Perkins (Photo taken by Robert McFarlane, 1963)

1. SAFA stands for ....

2. In 1965 the Mayor of Moree
   - A escalated the violence.
   - B threw rotten fruit at the Freedom Riders.
   - C supported the Segregationist Statute.
   - D enabled First Nations children to use the public swimming pool.

3. What do you think SAFA expected to find in country NSW?
   - A no evidence of racial discrimination
   - B evidence of racial discrimination
   - C fair treatment of First Nations people
   - D few First Nations people living there

4. Choose **all** that apply. In 1967 the referendum was carried, meaning that
   - A First Australians would be included in the census.
   - B federal funding was approved for towns in NSW.
   - C federal laws could be made specifically for First Australians.
   - D the states' powers to make laws specifically for First Nations people were removed.

5. The Freedom Ride was successful in that
   - A it visited Moree, Walgett and Dubbo.
   - B it hired a bus for touring the countryside.
   - C it drew attention to human-rights issues.
   - D it inspired events in America about racial discrimination.

6. How would most Australians feel now about a Segregationist Statute that prevented some members of a community from using the public swimming pool? Choose **all** that apply.
   - A outraged
   - B annoyed
   - C pleased
   - D justified
   - E horrified
   - F angry

Answers and explanations on page 123

SPELLING

Rewrite the misspelt words in questions 1–3.

1 Perkins was opposed to rashal discrimination. ....

2 The Segragationist Statue of 1955 was enforced. ....

3 The unaversity protesters were pelted with rotten fruit. ....

4 Add a prefix to this word from the text: **treatment**. Then write a definition for the new word. ....

....

5 Write three words from the word family that includes **investigate**.

....

VOCABULARY

6 Use a dictionary that includes word origins. Explain the origin and meaning of this word from the text: **Indigenous**.

7 Circle the answer that has the nearest meaning to the underlined word.

The Mayor intervened.

A interrupted B interfered
C interceded D intercepted

8 Choose the correct definition for this word from the text: **escalating**.

A improving B stopping
C lessening D increasing

9 Use a dictionary. Write a definition for this word from the text: **statute**.

....

....

Circle the word that does **not** belong.

10 A discrimination B inclusion
C prejudice D bias

11 A clash B confrontation
C protest D altercation

GRAMMAR

12 Circle the extended noun group that includes an adjectival clause.

Perkins was inspired by American events that highlighted discrimination.

13 Circle the modal verb that expresses the most certainty or obligation.

All people (should / must / could) be afforded the same rights.

14 Add a modal adverb that expresses certainty.

The 1967 referendum was .... supported by Australians.

15 Add a connective to complete the sentence.

The Freedom Riders were spat upon .... they were just trying to help First Nations children.

PUNCTUATION

16 Circle the sentence that is punctuated correctly.

A The bus which was hired by SAFA, set out from Sydney.
B The referendum, which was held in 1967, was supported by 90% of Australians.
C The bus drove, to Moree.

Rewrite each sentence correctly.

17 the group visited dubbo walgett moree tenterfield grafton lismore and kempsey

....

....

....

18 students from sydney university formed safa (student action for aborigines)

....

....

....

Answers and explanations on pages 123–124

 **Text 2**

Rights and freedoms

Human rights are rights that should be available to every human being, regardless of where in the world they live. These rights include the right to live freely; to be treated fairly; to live in safety without fear of persecution, torture or detainment; to have adequate food, water, medicine and shelter; to have an education; and to have a family.

Civil rights are rights granted to citizens by government. These rights vary greatly from one country to the next. Civil rights include workers' rights to fair pay, the right to a fair trial, freedom of the press and the right to vote.

Social justice means ensuring that every person in society has equitable access to running water, sanitation, education, employment, housing and health care.

The Australian Human Rights Commission stated in 2003 that social justice also means 'recognising the distinctive rights that Indigenous Australians hold as the original peoples of this land'.

Source: www.humanrights.gov.au/our-work/aboriginal-and-torres-strait-islander-social-justice/guides/information-sheet-social]

Australian postage stamp circa 2013 honouring Mum Shirl (1924–1998), social worker, humanitarian and activist. The 2013 stamp series featured First Australian leaders.

1 Choose **two** answers. Text 1 in Unit 25A and Text 2 use language that is

- **A** emotive.
- **B** objective.
- **C** factual.
- **D** biased.
- **E** poetic.

2 Human rights apply

- **A** when governments agree.
- **B** in some places only.
- **C** in most places.
- **D** to everyone.

3 Civil rights

- **A** are different everywhere.
- **B** are the same everywhere.
- **C** apply equitably in all countries.
- **D** are the same as human rights.

4 What special rights might First Nation Australians hold as 'the original peoples of this land' (line 13)? Choose **all** that apply.

- **A** land rights
- **B** the right to be recognised as the first Australians
- **C** the right to their own spiritual and cultural practices
- **D** the right to be treated fairly

5 How are Text 1 in Unit 25A and Text 2 related?

....

....

6 List the relevant topics in the columns. The first one has been done for you.

Human rights	*to live freely*
Civil rights	
Social justice	

7 Design a stamp to honour a well-known Australian of your choice.

Answers and explanations on page 124

READING AND COMPREHENSION

Text 1

Interview: Regenerative farming

Host: In our studio today we have regenerative farming proponent Thomas Gorrie. Thomas, thanks for joining us.

Thomas: Thank you for having me, Carmel. I'm happy to be here.

Host: Please explain to viewers what regenerative farming means.

Thomas: Sure. Years of land clearing and deforestation, intensive farming, chemical fertilisers and pesticide use causes soil to degrade. Degraded soil has lost all of its organic matter, the worms have gone and pests abound. Regenerative farming means using more ecological and sustainable methods of farming so that degraded soil can recover. We need to regenerate our soil because, just like the air, and the oceans and trees, soil also stores carbon. We don't want carbon in the air and we have too much already in the ocean so we need the trees and soil to store it safely. Degraded soil has reduced ability to store carbon, it's lost its ability to hold water, it grows less food and it requires more and more fertilisers, herbicides and pesticides.

Host: I hadn't thought about soil in that way.

Thomas: It's alarming what is being done to the soil all over the world in the name of food production. The science is irrefutable: composting, using organic fertiliser and crop rotation enhance the soil's ability to hold carbon, as well as improve crop yield and quality. We feed our soil and it feeds us. The science is truly exciting because soil can actively pull carbon from the atmosphere. Regenerative farming could play a very big part in helping the earth in relation to climate change. It's all about working with nature rather than against it.

Host: Why aren't all farms becoming regenerative then?

Thomas: Whenever short-term profit is involved and powerful companies such as fertiliser or pesticide producers have vested interests, it's difficult to get the environmental message through.

Host: Thank you, Thomas, for your insights. They are definitely food for thought. Pardon the pun!

1 Regenerative farming means
- **A** degrading the soil.
- **B** rehabilitating the soil.
- **C** re-energising the soil.
- **D** feeding the soil with organic compost.

2 How does healthy soil help climate change?
- **A** It grows more food.
- **B** It holds more water
- **C** It stores carbon.
- **D** It needs more chemicals.

3 Which statements are true according to Thomas?
- **A** Composting improves the soil.
- **B** Improved soil yields better crops.
- **C** Unhealthy soil has no worms.
- **D** Unhealthy soil cannot recover.
- **E** Healthy soil helps prevent climate change.

4 Thomas is .... regenerative farming.
- **A** opposed to
- **B** undecided about
- **C** supportive of
- **D** extremely supportive of

5 The host is
- **A** neutral.
- **B** biased towards Thomas's opinions.
- **C** biased against Thomas's opinions.

6 How is 'food for thought' (line 23) a pun?

....

....

....

Answers and explanations on page 124

SPELLING

Rewrite the misspelt words in questions 1–3.

1 Soil is ruined by defforestation.

2 Soil can activly pull carbon from the atmosphere.

3 Overuse of chemical fertalisers degrades the soil.

4 Add a prefix to this word from the text: **ability**. Then write a definition for the new word.

5 Write three words from the word family that includes **exciting**.

VOCABULARY

6 Use a dictionary that includes word origins. Explain the origin and meaning of this word from the text: **pesticide**.

7 Circle the answer that has the nearest meaning to the underlined word.

Soil can pull carbon from the <u>atmosphere</u>.

A air between the moon and the sun
B oxygen and carbon dioxide in the air
C the gases that surround the earth
D the mood of a story, film or poem

8 Choose the correct definition for this word from the text: **herbicide**.

A something that kills
B something that kills herbs
C something that's sprayed on weeds
D something that kills plants

9 Use a dictionary. Write a definition for this phrase from the text: **vested interest**.

Circle the word that does **not** belong.

10 A indisputable B controversial
C irrefutable D undeniable

11 A intensive B invasive
C concentrated D exhaustive

GRAMMAR

12 Circle the clause that describes **It**.

It is alarming what's being done to soil all over the world in the name of food.

13 Circle the modal verb that expresses the most certainty or obligation.

We really (must / should / could) eliminate waste.

14 Add a modal adverb that expresses certainty.

Your insights are .... food for thought.

15 Add a connective to complete the sentence.

.... degraded soil has no organic matter, it also has no worms.

PUNCTUATION

16 Circle the sentence that is punctuated correctly.

A Any questions, you have should be saved for later.
B Any questions you have should be saved for later.
C Save any questions, for later.

Rewrite each sentence correctly.

17 its important that soil maintains its quality

18 the soils ability to regenerate is amazing said thomas

Answers and explanations on page 124

TEXTS IN CONTEXT

Text 2

Farmers love sewage

Farmers on the Liverpool plains west of Sydney are having great success with the biosolids from Sydney's sewage treatment plants; so much success that demand for the product is increasing at a rate not able to be supplied by the residents of Sydney.

Household sewage is treated in the plants: the by-product, biosolids or treated solids are sold to farmers to improve their soil by adding organic matter to improve water retention, as well as adding essential nutrients such as copper, zinc, potassium, phosphorus and nitrogen.

Farmer Elaine Cooper has been using biosolids on her sheep farm to create healthy pastures for over five years now and is impressed with the benefits the resource has brought. 'It's really improved the yield and quality of my pastures and my sheep are much healthier and bigger as a result.'

There are strict government guidelines on the safe use of the biosolids in farms. Biosolids are ploughed into the soil and then stock and crops are withheld for specified periods.

Sydney Water is happy to send off trucks full of biosolids knowing that this protects the ocean. Creating the biosolids generates electricity as well, so it's a win-win for everyone. A conventional waste product has become a valuable commodity.

1 What is the structure of the interview in Text 1 (Unit 26A)?

- A introduce the guest, explain his background then discuss the topic
- B introduce and define the topic then explain degraded soil
- C introduce and define the topic then provide information
- D introduce the topic then give arguments for and against regenerative farming

2 What is the structure of Text 2?

- A lead paragraph then a feel-good story
- B lead paragraph, explanations in order of newsworthiness, interview quote
- C lead paragraph, newsworthy information, witness statement, conclusion
- D lead paragraph, information in order of newsworthiness, interview quote, conclusion

3 What are biosolids?

....

....

....

....

4 Choose **all** that apply. The tone of Text 1 (Unit 26A) is

A downbeat.	B disheartened.
C annoyed.	D optimistic.
E pessimistic.	F excited.

The tone of Text 2 is

A angry.	B positive.
C formal.	D disgusted.
E upbeat.	F downbeat.

5 What is the connection between Text 1 in Unit 26A and Text 2?

6 Elaine Cooper in Text 2 and Thomas Gorrie in Text 1 (Unit 26A)

- A have different backgrounds.
- B have the same goals.
- C agree in theory but not in practice.
- D have similar interests.

7 Search the internet for a photo that you think matches Text 2 better than the one provided. Explain your choice.

Answers and explanations on page 124

READING AND COMPREHENSION

Text 1

Fire burn and cauldron bubble

(a scene from *Macbeth* by William Shakespeare, first performed in 1606)

ACT 4 Scene 1

A cavern. In the middle, a boiling cauldron.
Thunder. Enter the three Witches

ALL:
Double, double toil and trouble;
Fire burn, and cauldron bubble.

SECOND WITCH:
Fillet of a fenny snake,
In the cauldron boil and bake;
Eye of newt and toe of frog,
Wool of bat and tongue of dog,
Adder's fork and blind-worm's sting,
Lizard's leg and owlet's wing,
For a charm of powerful trouble,
Like a hell-broth boil and bubble.

ALL:
Double, double toil and trouble;
Fire burn and cauldron bubble.

Enter HECATE

HECATE:
Oh well done! I commend your pains,
And every one shall share i' th' gains.
And now about the cauldron sing,
Like elves and fairies in a ring,
Enchanting all that you put in.

1 What are the witches doing?

2 What is an 'Adder's fork' (line 16)?

3 The witches want to
A burn things.
B eat snakes, frogs and dogs.
C cause trouble.
D sing and dance in a ring around the cauldron like elves and fairies.

4 What is Hecate's relationship to the witches?

5 'Enchanting all that you put in' (line 29).
What do you think this means?

6 Use evidence from the text to describe the atmosphere in Scene 1.

Answers and explanations on pages 124–125

SPELLING

Rewrite the misspelt words in questions 1–3.

1 Adders fork ....

2 blind-werms sting ....

3 tunge of dog ....

4 Add a prefix to this word from the text: **troubled**. Then write a definition for the new word.

....

5 Write three words from the word family that includes **power**.

....

....

VOCABULARY

6 Use a dictionary that includes word origins. Explain the origin and meaning of this word from the text: **cauldron**.

7 Circle the answer that has the nearest meaning to the underlined word.

Like a hell-broth

A a poisoned soup
B an unpleasant-tasting stew
C a magical soup
D a stew made for evil purposes

8 Choose the correct definition for this word from the text: **commend**.

A praise B command
C acknowledge D notice

9 Use a dictionary. Write a definition for this word from the text: **cavern**.

....

....

Circle the word that does **not** belong.

10 A trouble B mischief
C harmony D problems

11 A fillet B chop
C slice D strip

GRAMMAR

12 Circle the extended noun group that includes an adjectival clause.

Add the lizard's leg that had been chewed on by the cat.

13 Circle the modal verb that expresses the most certainty or obligation.

Everyone (might / could / shall) share the gains.

14 Add a modal adverb that expresses certainty.

Your ideas are .... worth considering.

15 Add a connective to complete the sentence.

.... biosolids improve soil by adding organic matter, they also add essential nutrients.

PUNCTUATION

16 Circle the sentence that is punctuated correctly.

A Hugos one of a kind.
B My brother Hugo's one of a kind
C Hugo, my brother is one of a kind.

Rewrite each sentence correctly.

17 well done declared hecate

....

....

18 its a blindworms sting said second witch

....

....

....

Answers and explanations on page 125

TEXTS IN CONTEXT

Text 2

Medusa

How did Medusa do her hair?
The question fills me with despair.
It must have caused her sore distress
That head of curling snakes to dress.
Whenever after endless toil
She coaxed it finally to coil,
The music of a Passing Band
Would cause each separate hair to stand
On end and sway and writhe and spit,—
She couldn't 'do a thing with it.'
And, being woman and aware
Of such disaster to her hair,
What could she do but petrify
All whom she met, with freezing eye?

From *The Mythological Zoo* by Oliver Herford, 1912

1 Medusa has .... for hair.

2 In Text 1 (Unit 27A) Hecate says, 'Oh well done! I commend your pains, And every one shall share i' th' gains.' What does Hecate mean?

....

....

....

3 Find and write an example of each of the following from either Text 1 in Unit 27A or Text 2:

Assonance

....

Simile

....

Rhyme

....

Alliteration

....

4 What happened to Medusa's hair when music was played?

....

....

5 What does Text 2 imply about attitudes to women in 1912? Explain, using evidence from the text.

....

....

6 How are Text 1 in Unit 27A and Text 2 related? Find at least **four** ways.

....

....

....

....

Get creative

7 Write a poem based on a mythological being.

Answers and explanations on page 125

READING AND COMPREHENSION

 Text 1

Valuing language

English is a living language. A living language changes with use. It expands and grows, new words and phrases are coined, words drop from common usage, and word meanings evolve and change.

Latin is a dead language. A dead language has no native speakers. Latin was the language of Rome in 750 BC but by around 750 AD it was dead. Today only a few scholars can speak Latin but it can still be studied and used in certain contexts. Many English words, including the names of animals, plants and medical and scientific terms, have Greek or Latin roots. For example, *Canis* is Latin for dog. Canine is an adjective that relates to dogs. Canine teeth are the pointed teeth of carnivores. Carnivore is from the Latin *carnivorus*, which means flesh-eating. Other dead languages include Sanskrit, Aramaic and Coptic. Language carries invaluable cultural and historical knowledge and identity, and ways of being and seeing the world.

Extinct languages are languages that were lost when their last speakers died. Many languages are in danger of extinction as people replace their native languages with English or other modern languages. Communities do this out of necessity or the fear of marginalisation. They adopt the language of the dominant group in order to survive economically, to get a job or an education, or to avoid discrimination. Then the native languages become extinct.

It is sometimes possible to revive an extinct language by introducing it to a new generation of speakers who can then pass the language down to the next generation. It requires a major effort to achieve success in reviving an extinct or endangered language. Ninety per cent of Australia's Indigenous languages are critically endangered. A number of community groups and universities are mapping and recording as many of these languages as possible in the hope of saving them. There are also programs underway to teach them in schools.

Carpe diem is a Latin phrase, colloquially translated to mean seize the day.

1 Why do people study dead languages?
- A because they need to get a job
- B because they give insight into culture and identity
- C because they are useful at university
- D so they can converse with others

2 How does a language become extinct?

....

3 Latin is a dead language because it
- A is only used by scholars.
- B was alive in Roman times.
- C has no native speakers.
- D is rarely used.

4 If someone says *Carpe diem* to you, what do they mean?
- A Take today as it comes.
- B Grab each day in a row.
- C Make the most of every day.
- D Live a full and happy life.

5 Which occupations might most benefit from an understanding of Greek and Latin word roots?
- A salespeople
- B doctors
- C horticulturalists
- D plumbers
- E vets

6 Choose **all** that apply. Imagine living somewhere where businesses, schools and government only used English but English was your second language. How might you feel?
- A proud
- B unimportant
- C unvalued
- D marginalised
- E important

Answers and explanations on page 125

SPELLING

Rewrite the misspelt words in questions 1–3.

1 Many Indiginous languages are endangered. ....

2 Many languages are criticly endangered.

....

3 Many sientific terms have Latin roots.

....

4 Add a prefix to this word from the text: **valuable**. Then write a definition for the new word.

....

5 Write three words from the word family that includes **cultural**.

....

VOCABULARY

6 Use a dictionary that includes word origins. Explain the origin and meaning of this word from the text: **communities.**

7 Circle the answer that has the nearest meaning to the underlined word.

Words and phrases are <u>coined.</u>

A invented **B** spelt
C written down **D** added to dictionaries

8 Choose the correct definition for this word from the text: **revive**.

A wake up **B** become conscious
C resuscitate **D** recover

9 Use a dictionary. Write a definition for this word from the text: **marginalisation**.

....

....

Circle the word that does **not** belong.

10 **A** avoid **B** evade
C dodge **D** escape

11 **A** evolve **B** regress
C develop **D** grow

GRAMMAR

12 Circle the clause that describes this word from the text: ***carnivorus***.

Carnivore is from the Latin *carnivorus*, which means flesh-eating,

13 Circle the modal verb that expresses the least certainty.

It (might / can / won't) be possible to revive an endangered language.

14 Circle the modal adverb that expresses the least certainty.

Aunty could (possibly / potentially / probably) teach me her language.

15 Add a connective to complete the sentence.

Mum and Jack are still deciding if I can take guitar lessons. ...., I will keep nagging them.

PUNCTUATION

16 Circle the sentence that is punctuated correctly.

A Ninety per cent of Australia's Indigenous languages are critically endangered.
B More than half of English word's are from Greek or Latin.
C The Roman's spoke Latin in 750 BC.

Rewrite each sentence correctly.

17 Im not a carnivore am I asked saxon

....

....

18 carpe diem said harriet

....

....

Answers and explanations on page 125

Text 2

English—a living language

English is a living language. It is constantly changing, growing and evolving. New words and phrases are added on a regular basis because of usage, technology, inventions, discoveries, literature, advertising and borrowings from other languages.

A noun can become a verb: I'll message you when I get there. I'll text you later.

An adjective can become a noun: She's a Green.

Young people use slang words: cool; hip; deadly.

Authors invent words in literary texts: triantiwontigongalope, muggles.

Words are borrowed from other languages: sushi (Japan); smorgasbord (Sweden); shampoo (soap for the hair from India); banana (from the African Congo region but originally from Arabic).

Words can be composites: motor + hotel = motel; breakfast + lunch = brunch.

Advertising adds new words: Bandaid®, Kleenex®. (® means that the company or product name is legally registered.)

Words can be acronyms: radar (radio detecting and ranging).

Technology changes how words are used: c u l8ter; lol.

Some words develop new meanings: a mouse is a small mammal but also something used with a computer.

1 What is a carnivore in Text 1 (Unit 28A)?
- **A** a mammal
- **B** an animal with pointed teeth
- **C** a dog
- **D** an animal that eats meat

2 Why are people working to preserve endangered languages (Text 1, Unit 28A)?

....

....

3 Why are Kleenex and Bandaid special words?

....

....

4 Talk with a friend or family member. List words in English that have come from other languages.

....

....

5 Which words do you use with friends that are not necessarily part of your family's usual way of speaking? List them here.

....

....

6 How is Text 1 in Unit 28A related to Text 2?

....

....

....

Get creative

7 Create a picture book for young children that uses words from an endangered First Nation Australian language.

Answers and explanations on page 125

READING AND COMPREHENSION

 **Text 1**

War

People killed or maimed or
scarred on the inside
where it's harder to see
but can't be hidden.
Military, civilians, children,
babies.

Animals suffer,
infrastructure demolished;
the environment ruined;
our planet scarred;
advancing technology
making the devastation worse.

Terms for war:
inter-nation and intra-nation;
civil, revolutionary, cold,
armed conflicts, insurgencies and guerrilla
warfare,
the war on terror, race wars, the war on drugs;
World Wars.

Wars fought for land or religion.
Wars fought for resources—oil, diamonds, water.
Wars fought over politics or ideals,
or in the name of colonialism or racism.
Pre-emptive wars—
striking first so you don't get struck.

The aftermath of grief and loss—
families decimated;
cities in ruins, roads and bridges gone;
farmland now planted with landmines.
Destruction can arrive quickly—
rebuilding takes lifetimes.
How much do we spend on peace?

Peace Memorial Garden, Hiroshima

1. List the reasons for war mentioned by the poet.

2. 'advancing technology making the devastation worse' (lines 12–13)
   What does this mean?

3. 'scarred on the inside / where it's harder to see / but can't be hidden' (lines 3–5)
   What does this mean?

4. 'farmland now planted with landmines' (line 30)
   What is the impact of this?

5. What is the implication of the final question (line 33)?

6. 'rebuilding takes lifetimes' (line 32)
   Explain this line in the poem.

Answers and explanations on page 126

SPELLING

Rewrite the misspelt words in questions 1–3.

1 Our planet is scared. ....

2 An insergency is a kind of war. ....

3 People fight over religon. ....

4 Add a prefix to this word from the text: **national**. Then write a definition for the new word.

....

5 Write three words from the word family that includes **demolished**.

....

VOCABULARY

6 Use a dictionary that includes word origins. Explain the origin and meaning of this word from the text: **guerrilla**.

7 Circle the answer that has the nearest meaning to the underlined word.

War can be intranational.

- A involving all nations
- B in the interests of nations
- C between two nations
- D within one nation

8 Choose the correct definition for this phrase from the text: **civil war**.

- A a war that is polite
- B a war between neighbours
- C a war between people within a country
- D a war between politicians

9 Use a dictionary. Write a definition for this word from the text: **colonialism**.

....

....

Circle the word that does **not** belong.

10 A appropriate B pre-emptive C deterrent D preventative

11 A devastation B rebuilding C desolation D ruins

GRAMMAR

12 Circle the clause that describes the **civil war**.

The civil war, a devastating, decade-long battle which cost thousands of lives, has come to an end.

13 Circle the modal verb that expresses the least certainty.

The cafe (could / must / might) have closed because it's after 9 pm.

14 Circle the modal adverb that expresses the least certainty

It's (obviously / probably / crucially) important to provide aid to refugees.

15 Add a connective to complete the sentence.

I have donated to the charity already. ...., I could always donate more.

PUNCTUATION

16 Circle the sentence that is punctuated correctly.

- A War does not discriminate between military, civilians, children, and babies.
- B World war II lasted from 1939 to 1945.
- C The Peace Memorial Garden is in Hiroshima.

Rewrite each sentence correctly.

17 the prime minister announced a war on drugs

....

....

18 we wont commit to this war declared the minister for defence

....

....

Answers and explanations on page 126

TEXTS IN CONTEXT

Text 2

The Nobel Prize

The Nobel Prize is named for Alfred Nobel, a Swedish chemist. He invented dynamite among other achievements. In 1896 when he died he left his money in a bequest to honour achievements in chemistry, physics, physiology/medicine, literature and peace. An Economics Prize was added in 1968. The Nobel Prize is administered by the Nobel Foundation in Sweden. Recipients receive a medal, a diploma and money. Nobel prize winners are called Laureates. The term laureate comes from the laurel wreaths used in ancient Greece to honour victors.

Nobel Prize winners have included Rudyard Kipling—Literature, 1907; Marie Curie—Physics, 1903 and Chemistry, 1911; Albert Einstein—Physics, 1921; and Martin Luther King Jr—Peace, 1964.

The 2014 Nobel Peace Prize was awarded to Malala Yousafzai. Malala was 17 when she was awarded the Prize for her work for children's rights, girls' rights and the right of all children to an education.

In 2017 the Nobel Peace Prize was awarded to ICAN, the International Campaign for the Abolition of Nuclear Weapons. ICAN is a coalition of non-government organisations from over 100 countries. It began in Australia in 2017. It was awarded the Peace Prize for its 'work to draw attention to the catastrophic humanitarian consequences of any use of nuclear weapons and for its groundbreaking efforts to achieve a treaty-based prohibition of such weapons.' (www.nobelprize.org/nobel_prizes/peace/laureates/2017/press.html)

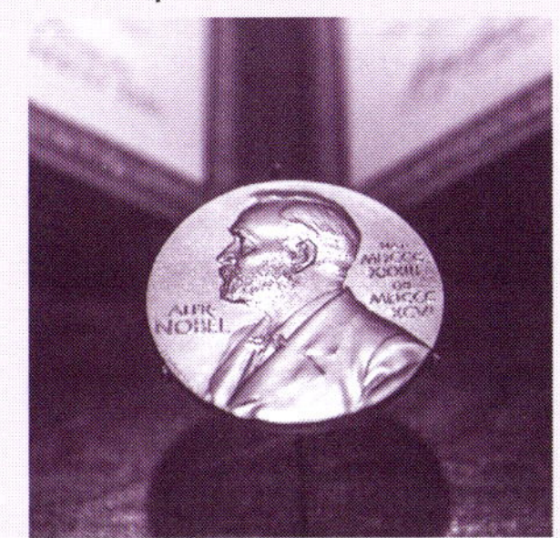

The Nobel medals show the image of Alfred Nobel. The image on the reverse varies according to the institution awarding the prize.

Accepting the award on behalf of ICAN were Beatrice Fihn and Setsuko Thurlow. (Setsuko survived the Hiroshima atomic bomb when she was 13 years old.) On accepting the award Beatrice Fihn said, 'If only a small fraction of today's nuclear weapons were used, soot and smoke from the firestorms would loft high into the atmosphere—cooling, darkening and drying the Earth's surface for more than a decade. It would obliterate food crops, putting billions at risk of starvation.'

1. Nobel prize winners are called .... They receive a .... , a .... and ....

2. A laurel wreath signifies ....

3. Find and write emotive words used in Text 2.

   ....

   ....

4. What is the writer's purpose in including the two quotes in Text 2?

   ....

   ....

5. How are Text 1 in Unit 29A and Text 2 related?

   ....

   ....

6. How would Setsuko feel about nuclear weapons? Explain.

   ....

   ....

Get creative

7. Research a Nobel Prize Laureate of your choice. Write a report.

Answers and explanations on page 126

 Text 1

Conscription

Conscription is when a government forces its citizens to serve in the military. Conscription is sometimes deemed necessary by governments when there are not enough volunteers freely enlisting to fight in wars or to take the places of injured or dead soldiers.

Conscription for overseas service was not approved by Australian voters in referendums held during WWI (in 1916 and again in 1917); however, it was used to send young men to New Guinea during WWII. It was abolished in 1959 but reintroduced for the Vietnam War. The government passed the National Service Act of 1964 whereby young men, selected by a ballot of birthdates, were forced into National Service (drafted) and required to serve for two years. There were many peace protests in Australian capital cities during this time. In 1965 the Defence Act was amended so that the conscripted men could be sent overseas to fight.

There were 60 000 Australian soldiers in Vietnam: 15 381 of those were conscripted; 200 of the 521 dead were conscripts and 1279 of the 3000 wounded were conscripts.

Conscripted men who did not want to go to war became conscientious objectors. Some went to jail rather than fight in a war they did not agree with. When the Vietnam War ended, seven young men were still in jail. They were freed at the end of 1972. Conscription was abolished, by law, in 1973. To reintroduce it at any future date will require approval of both the Senate and the House of Representatives.

The Vietnam War was an unpopular war with many Australians who believed Australians should not have been involved in it. When soldiers returned from Vietnam they did not get a heroes' welcome. They were unfairly stigmatised because of their involvement in the war. Some became socially isolated and suffered post-traumatic stress disorder (PTSD).

Government recruitment poster used during WWI

1 Why do governments use conscription?

....

2 List **two** ways in which people went overseas to fight in wars.

....

....

3 What is the writer's attitude to conscription?

A neutral
B supportive
C opposed
D supportive when deemed necessary by the government

4 What reasons could a conscientious objector have for refusing to be conscripted?

....

....

5 Would you judge Australians as generally pro- or anti-conscription? Explain using evidence in the text.

....

....

....

6 The poster assumes that young men will want to fight for God and country. What could be wrong with this assumption?

....

....

....

....

Answers and explanations on page 126

SPELLING

Rewrite the misspelt words in questions 1–3.

1 3000 solders were injured. ....

2 Some men became conscientius objectors.

....

3 The Defense Act was amended in 1965.

....

4 Add a prefix to this word from the text: **introduced**. Then write a definition for the new word.

....

5 Write three words from the word family that includes **volunteer**.

....

VOCABULARY

6 Use a dictionary that includes word origins. Explain the origin and meaning of this word from the text: **conscription**.

7 Circle the answer that has the nearest meaning to the underlined word.

Soldiers were unfairly <u>stigmatised</u>.

A regarded as shameful
B marked for humiliation
C treated
D conscripted

8 Choose the correct definition for this word from the text: **referendum**.

A an issue that needs people's votes
B a matter referred to experts
C a vote by the people
D a vote in parliament

9 Use a dictionary. Write a definition for this noun group from the text: **post-traumatic stress disorder**.

....

Circle the word that does **not** belong.

10 A amended B revised C modified D unedited

11 A shunned B popular C unpopular D disliked

GRAMMAR

12 Circle the clause that describes **war**.

Some went to jail rather than fight in a war they did not agree with.

13 Circle the modal verb that expresses the least certainty.

It rained while we were on holiday so the garden (must / should / will) be fine.

14 Circle the modal adverb that expresses the least certainty.

I (completely / unreservedly / potentially) agree with your answer.

15 Add a connective to complete the sentence.

Potato chips are unhealthy because they are high in salt. .... they are high in fat.

PUNCTUATION

16 Circle the sentence that is punctuated correctly.

A Low-flying Drones can be used in warfare.
B Elton John (born Reginald Dwight) turned 75 in 2022.
C Noomi opened a high-interest savings Account.

Rewrite each sentence correctly.

17 Id be a conscientious objector declared aaron

....

....

18 returning vietnam veterans did not receive a heroes welcome in the 1970s

....

....

Answers and explanations on page 127

TEXTS IN CONTEXT

Text 2

Our excursion

Our class went on an excursion to the Australian War Memorial. We participated in the Vietnam Era program. It was really worthwhile and I learned more from our presenter than I would have learned if I had just wandered around the museum with my classmates.

I learned that propaganda is a powerful tool that has been used throughout history to influence people's opinions and perceptions. War propaganda promotes nationalism and uses scare tactics to make people fearful of the enemy and what the enemy might do.

I learned that Australia's participation in the Vietnam War was contentious. There were big protests in Australia about the war. Many posters were produced, some by the government supporting the war effort and some by objectors opposing Australia's involvement in the war and opposing conscription. Posters were cheap to make and easy to distribute. Propaganda posters were also successfully used by the Vietnamese.

The Australian War Memorial

1 The purpose of the poster shown in Text 1 (Unit 30A) is to

A inform. B entertain.
C describe a war. D persuade.
E present an opinion. F recount events.

2 The purpose of Text 2 is to

A inform. B entertain.
C describe a war. D persuade.
E present an opinion. F recount events.

3 The intended audience for Text 1 in Unit 30A would be

A military experts.
B ordinary people with an interest in the history of conscription.
C young men who might get conscripted.
D members of the government.

4 What evidence in Text 2 tells readers that the writer would likely recommend this excursion?

....

....

....

5 What do you think a poster would need to show today to encourage young people to enlist in the Defence Force? Explain.

....

....

....

....

6 What would an anti-war propaganda poster show?

....

....

....

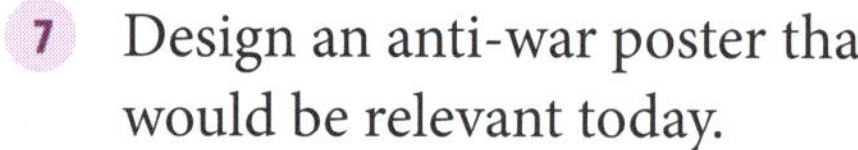

7 Design an anti-war poster that would be relevant today.

Answers and explanations on page 127

 Text 1

Thomas Edison (1847–1931)

Inventor of the phonograph, the incandescent light bulb and a motion-picture camera, Thomas Edison was labelled a hyperactive and difficult child by his first school teachers so his mother, who had been a teacher, decided to homeschool him. Throughout his life Edison had a voracious appetite for learning and knowledge, and was an avid reader.

At age 15 he became a telegraph operator and this occupation would lead to some of his future inventions and interests.

At age 22 Edison invented a machine for use on the stock market and was paid $40 000 for the patent. The money allowed him to quit work as a telegraph operator and focus on inventing things, mostly for Western Union Telegraph Company. For example, he developed the quadruplex telegraph for telegraphing messages in different directions on the same wire at the same time.

At age 29 he set up his own research facility employing many other inventors and scientists, including Nikola Tesla* and Francis R Upton**.

At age 30, in 1877, he developed the phonograph, a method of recording and reproducing sound. It took a further ten years to make it a commercial success. This invention gave Edison international acclaim.

Edison took the light-bulb inventions of other inventors from around the word and improved on their designs to make the first commercially practical light bulb in 1880. He then focused on meter electricity usage and on improving methods of electricity generation. He founded the Edison Illuminating Company, which later became the General Electric Corporation.

His other inventions included a motion-picture camera and the alkaline storage battery. Edison was a prolific inventor throughout his life and patented over 1000 inventions.

*Tesla only worked for Edison briefly and went on to develop his own inventions of electrical, mechanical and wireless devices.
**Upton worked for Edison from 1878 to 1911 and was instrumental in the development of the light bulb, among other inventions. Upton and fellow inventor, Fernando J Dibble, invented the portable electric fire alarm and detector, patented in 1890

 Text 2

Thomas Edison—A Great Inventor

Note: This children's book has a new paragraph for every sentence and other unusual formatting.

Thomas A. Edison was born in Milan, Ohio, February 11, 1847.

He went to a regular school only two months.

His father and mother were his teachers.

His father, to encourage him to read, paid him for every book which he read.

But Thomas did not need to be paid to read, for he read with pleasure every volume he could get hold of.

When he was ten years old, he was reading such books as Gibbon's 'History of Rome,' Hume's 'History of England,' and Sear's 'History of the World.'

Besides these, he had read several books about chemistry.

He loved to read about great men and their deeds.

When he played, it was at building plank roads, digging caves, and exploring the banks of the canal.

When only twelve years of age, he was obliged to go out into the world and earn his own living.

He obtained a place as train-boy on the Grand Trunk Railroad, in Eastern Michigan.

He sold apples, peanuts, song-books, and [news]papers.

He had such a pleasant, sunny face that everyone liked to buy of him.

He succeeded so well that soon he had four boys working under him.

This was not enough to keep him busy.

He had never lost his liking for chemistry.

He managed to trade some of his [news]papers for things with which to try experiments.

He found a book which helped him.

Source: from *Project Gutenberg's Stories of Great Inventors* by Hattie E Macomber, 1897

1 Which statement is true of Edison?
- A He read books his mother chose for him.
- B He read for enjoyment and learning.
- C His father had to pay him to read.
- D He only read books about inventions.

2 Upton and Dibble in Text 1 invented
- A a light bulb.
- B a fire alarm.
- C a motion-picture camera.
- D the phonograph.

3 Choose **all** that apply. Which commercial companies are listed in Text 1?
- A the quadruplex telegraph
- B General Electric Corporation
- C Edison Illuminating Company
- D Western Union Telegraph Company

4 Choose **all** that apply. What can you infer from Texts 1 and 2 about Edison's likely attitude to school?
- A He wanted to learn but the teachers did not like him.
- B He did not like sitting in a classroom.
- C The classroom did not teach what he was interested in.
- D He was bored and disliked it.

5 Edison's first business venture (age 12) was a success because ....

....

6 Tick the boxes. Which are true?

	Text 1		Text 2	
	True	False	True	False
A Edison showed his passion for learning from a young age.	☐	☐	☐	☐
B Edison was a hard worker.	☐	☐	☐	☐
C Edison created his own inventions.	☐	☐	☐	☐
D Edison sometimes improved the inventions of others.	☐	☐	☐	☐
E Inventors compete with each other to invent things.	☐	☐	☐	☐

7 Text 2 is written for
- A children.
- B adults.
- C people interested in science.
- D people who read in trains.

8 The phrase 'voracious appetite for learning' (line 5) in Text 1 means
- A devouring things too greedily.
- B always hungry to learn.
- C eating fiercely like a lion.
- D a big appetite that's never satisfied.

9 What evidence tells readers that some inventions are not commercial successes?

....

....

....

10 Texts 1 and 2 are similar because
- A they tell the story of Edison's childhood.
- B they describe Edison's home life and schooling.
- C they describe Edison's relationships with other inventors.
- D they include biographical information.

11 What was special about Edison's invention of the phonograph?

....

....

....

12 'He loved to read about great men and their deeds' (Text 2, line 11).

What does this tell you about Edison?

....

....

....

Answers and explanations on page 127

The incorrect word in each sentence has been circled. Write the correct spelling of each word.

1 Edison invented the (incandesent) light bulb.

2 He made the first (commercialy) practical light bulb.

3 He was a (proliffic) inventor.

4 Upton was instrumental in (develeping) the light bulb.

5 Edison later (focessed) on ways to generate electricity.

6 Dibble patented a fire (detecter).

7 Choose the correct answer to complete the sentence.

Edison's teacher found him disruptive so his mother homeschooled ....

A her B he
C them D him

8 In which sentence is **search** used as a verb?
A The search lasted a decade.
B He believed the search was worthwhile.
C The police had a search warrant.
D Let's search under the house.

9 Which word tells where the action happens?

He used the library after school.

A He
B used
C library
D school

10 Circle the theme of the sentence.

The incandescent light bulb was an important invention.

11 Circle the verbs or verb groups.

Thomas was a voracious reader, especially of books about great deeds and chemistry.

12 Which sentence shows the most certainty?
A Scientific developments might have improved people's lives.
B Scientific developments likely improved people's lives.
C Scientific developments have definitely been vital in improving people's lives.
D Scientific developments have really improved people's lives.

13 Which adverbial completes the sentence correctly?

He developed the light bulb ....

A among other inventions.
B towards other inventions.
C from other inventions.
D amongst other inventions.

14 Underline the independent (main) clause in the sentence.

He found a book which helped him.

15 Which sentence needs quotation marks (' and ') to enclose direct speech?
A Thomas asked to read the book.
B Thomas thought about his next invention.
C Thomas said he would like to work with electrical appliances.
D Thomas called out I've done it!

16 Which sentence is punctuated correctly?
A Mum always says 'to turn off the lights.'
B 'Don't waste electricity,' said Georgie.
C 'We'll need one light or its too dark,' said Fran.
D Bertie said 'he can't cook in the dark'.

Answers and explanations on page 127

ANSWERS

Unit 1A PAGE 8

1. **B**. See lines 11–12.
2. **D**. See lines 6–7.
3. **C**. You can infer that large batteries can store ample energy for use when the wind doesn't blow and the sun doesn't shine.
4. **A**, **B** and **C**. You can infer that improved technology supports a reliable and cheaper electricity supply.
5. **D**. You can judge that the photo is of a wind farm because it shows wind turbines.
6. **A**. You can judge that Ross Garnaut's opinion is respected because he is quoted in the article as an Australian economist.

Unit 1B PAGE 9

1. renewable
2. technology
3. superpower
4. undeveloped: not developed
5. Suggested answers: electric, electrical, electrifying, electrocuted, electronic, electrician
6. from the Latin *emergere* meaning rise out
7. **C**.
8. **A**.
9. a nation that has the ability to sell vast amounts of energy resources to the rest of the world
10. **B**.
11. **B**.
12. e.g. great, renewable, energy
13. A can be stored; does not fail
    B means; does not fail
14. **D**.
15. when; Wind is a great source of renewable energy
16. **A**.
17. Australia has plenty of sun and wind.
18. 'Large-scale battery storage is important for the future,' announced Ross Garnaut.

Unit 1C PAGE 10

1. **D**.
2. **B**.
3. **C**.
4. International National Trusts Organisation (INTO)
5. **A**.
6. **D**. (**C** is true but is not the best answer.)
7. Responses will vary.

Unit 2A PAGE 11

1. **C**. See lines 16–17.
2. **B**. See line 16.
3. **A**. You can infer that because Babette wants to get to her 'true destination' she needs to concentrate so she can travel on.
4. **C** and **D**.
5. You can judge that if Babette scratches her nose she will lose concentration, the ground will crumble under her and she will fall into the ravine or end up at home without the book or her suitcase, and no way to start over.
6. You can judge that Babette travels by magic when she concentrates on reading her book. She seems to travel through space and time.

Unit 2B PAGE 12

1. suitcase
2. scratch
3. concentration
4. incomplete: unfinished, not complete
5. thought, thoughtful, thoughtless, think, unthinking
6. from the Latin *calumnia* meaning false accusation; also from the Middle English *chalange* and the Old French *chalenge*
7. **C**.
8. **B**.
9. break into pieces
10. **D**.
11. **B**.
12. e.g. solid wooden, sturdy plastic
13. A had to collect; had eluded
    B had eluded
14. **B**.
15. if; She could end up back home
16. **B**.
17. The first, second and third charms had been fairly easy for Babette to collect.
18. Babette knew she had to collect all the charms.

Unit 2C PAGE 13

1. **D**.
2. **C**.
3. **A**, **D** and **E**.
4. **B**, **C** and **D**.
5. **C**.
6. Texts 1 and 2 are related in that Text 1 is an example of a particular genre and Text 2 shares children's reasons for enjoying different genres.
7. Responses will vary.

Unit 3A PAGE 14

1. **B**. See lines 12–20.
2. **C**. See lines 8–9.
3. **B**. You can infer that they squirmed because they were uncomfortable about a trick that they felt was not of a good standard ('lame').

4. **A**. You can infer that oohing and aahing is done when an audience is impressed.
5. **C**. You can judge that when the audience realised the magician was really missing then there was nothing to clap for.
6. **B**. You can judge that overall the writer was pretty impressed by the magician.

Unit 3B PAGE 15

1. magician
2. announced
3. audience
4. disappeared: vanished
5. Suggested answers: visibility, invisible, invisibility
6. from the Latin *finalis* meaning final
7. **B**.
8. **B**.
9. died out
10. **D**.
11. **C**.
12. e.g. simple, clever, amazing, card, vanishing, rope, coin
13. A announced; made
    B made
14. **C**.
15. when; Nobody was impressed
16. **A**.
17. 'Where's he gone?' asked Oli.
18. He'd indeed vanished into thin air.

Unit 3C PAGE 16

1. **B**.
2. **B**.
3. **D**.
4. **B**.
5. **C**.
6. **A** and **C**.
7. Responses will vary.

Unit 4A PAGE 17

1. **D**. See lines 5–6.
2. **A**, **B** and **C**. See lines 4–10.
3. **A**. You can infer that people pay to visit museums to see exhibits that show what life was like in the past.
4. **A** and **C**. You can infer that Tilda is afraid of ghosts because she hopes the castle isn't haunted. Tilda is only staying for the school holidays so her time in the castle is temporary.
5. **C**. You can judge that it was not totally safe inside the castle grounds if the enemy succeeded in breaching the walls, but it was safer than being out in the fields. The term 'relative' is used to relate one thing to another.
6. **B**. You can judge that she is interested because she imagines what life would have been like for her ancestors and is excited about the castle.

Unit 4B PAGE 18

1. ancestors
2. surrounding
3. furniture
4. unexciting: not exciting
5. Suggested answers: century, centurion, centenary, centennial, bicentennial
6. from the Latin *centuria* meaning a unit made up of 100 parts, e.g. 100 years in a century
7. **C**.
8. **A**.
9. a protective wall around the top of a castle
10. **C**.
11. **C**.
12. e.g. sturdy, secure, stone, castle
13. A approached; sounded; to hurry
    B approached; told to hurry
14. **A**.
15. because; Tilda hoped the castle wasn't haunted
16. **B**.
17. 'I hope the castle isn't haunted,' declared Tilda.
18. Tilda's ancestors were from Scotland.

Unit 4C PAGE 19

1. **A**.
2. **C**.
3. **A**, **B**, **C** and **D**.
4. **C**.
5. **B**.
6. **D**.
7. Responses will vary.

Unit 5A PAGE 20

1. **A**. See lines 9–11.
2. **B**. See line 3.
3. **B**. You can infer that any animal eating the bait will die, along with animals eating dead animals that have eaten the bait.
4. **C**. You can infer that native species are in decline because the red fox hunts and kills these smaller animals.
5. **A**. You can judge that foxes kill a variety of native animals because the text says the red fox kills native animals '**including** the greater bilby, the bridled nail-tail wallaby, the green turtle and ground-nesting birds such as the night parrot'.
6. **D**. You can judge that the text supports the use of 1080 because the government uses the poison and judges it necessary.

Unit 5B PAGE 21

1. government
2. boundaries
3. Residents
4. reassessed: assessed again

ANSWERS

5. Suggested answers: systematic, systematically, systemic
6. from the Dharug walaba meaning small kangaroo, from the language of the Dharug people of Western Sydney
7. **B**.
8. **C**.
9. a forest area owned and managed by a state government
10. **C**.
11. **B**.
12. e.g. poisonous bait, cruel poisonous
13. **A** will commence setting
    B will commence
14. **D**.
15. that; Neighbouring residents are warned; the traps will contain 1080 poison
16. **C**.
17. The European red fox is an introduced species.
18 'Traps will be set on 3 July,' announced Mayor Wu.

Unit 5C PAGE 22

1. **D**. The text informs about the problems with 1080 use. It does not instruct (**A**). It does not give alternative viewpoints (**B**). It is not a persuasive text because it neither includes a call to action nor tells people not to use 1080.
2. **B**.
3. **C**. (evil, cruelty, slow and agonising death, painful death)
4. **A** and **C**.
5. **D**.
6. **A** and **B**.
7. Responses will vary.

Unit 6A PAGE 23

1. **C**. See lines 6–7.
2. **D**. See lines 16–17.
3. **A**.
4. **C**. You can infer that it was written by a conservation organisation concerned about the extent of logging.
5. **A**, **B** and **D**.
6. **B**. You can judge that the writer opposes logging in old-growth forests.

Unit 6B PAGE 24

1. biodiversity
2. Environmental
3. canopy
4. mismanagement: manage badly or ineptly
5. Suggested answers: unavailable, availability, avail
6. from the Guugu Yimidhirr dhigul meaning a small marsupial, from the language of the Guugu Yimidhirr people of Far North Queensland
7. **D**.
8. **B**.
9. the cultivation of a single crop
10. **A**.
11. **C**.
12. e.g. huge, ancient, gum, fig
13. **A** are being cleared; destroys
    B destroys
14. **D**.
15. protect; ensuring; The old trees protect the ecosystem beneath their canopies
16. **A**.
17. 'Can we save Australia's old-growth forests?' asked Yelena.
18. Species such as gliders, possums, quolls, bats and owls need tree hollows.

Unit 6C PAGE 25

1. Suggested answers: valued, beauty, importance, survival, despair, lost forever, destroying
2. Suggested answers: Forest of Dread, unnaturally quiet, unscathed, doom, doomed, survive
3. The forest seemed to be holding its breath; the forest would judge whether Elon was pure of heart
4. traverse—travel through; unscathed—uninjured; dread—fear or apprehension; doomed— destined for something bad to happen; strode—walked purposefully
5. **A**, **B** and **C**.
6. **B** and **C**.
7. Responses will vary.

Unit 7A PAGE 26

1. **C**. See lines 9–10.
2. **C**. See lines 5, 13 and 20.
3. **D**. When you read the note you can tell its meaning is a puzzle so you can infer that cryptic means unclear or puzzling.
4. **B**. You can infer that Rose needs to read the headstones to find the correct one.
5. **A**, **B**, **C** and **D**. Evidence in the text suggests that each answer is likely true.
6. You can judge that Rose is bold, determined, hopeful and confident. You can judge that Grace is cautious, loyal, practical and cynical.

Unit 7B PAGE 27

1. phantoms
2. inaudible
3. character
4. impatient: not patient
5. audibility, auditory, inaudible, audibly, audibleness
6. probably from the Italian *basamento* meaning base
7. **C**.
8. **D**.
9. a gift of property or money, by will or as a bequest; something handed down by an ancestor or predecessor
10. **D**.

ANSWERS

11. **B**.
12. e.g. foggy, bleak, dawn, morning
13. **A** had discovered; written; gave
    B written; gave
14. **C**.
15. had left, died; Old Elijah had left an envelope
16. **B**.
17. It was like Rose's worst nightmare.
18. The bleak, biting cold only made it worse.

Unit 7C PAGE 28

1. **A**, **B** and **D**.
2. **C**.
3. like something from Rose's worst nightmare
4. In Text 1 Rose imagines phantoms (ghosts) because of the eeriness of the fog. In Text 2 the buildings look ghostlike through the fog.
5. **B**, **C**, **D** and **E**.
6. **C** and **A**.
7. Responses will vary.

NAPLAN-style Reading Test 1 PAGES 29–30

1. Text 1: to inform
   Text 2: to persuade
2. **B**, **C** and **D**.
3. **A** and **C**.
4. **B**.
5. **A**, **B**, **D**, **E** and **F**.
6. **B**.
7. **B**.
8. **C**.
9. Asking questions engages the reader or listener. Everyone will answer yes so it's more likely they will say yes to purchasing the product.
10. all their problems to be cured
11. Suggested answers: Greed: They think they will get money. Fear: They fear that something bad will happen if they don't do what is asked. Kindness: They think they are helping someone. Trust: They trust that the person scamming them is being truthful. Hope: They hope that what they are being told is true.
12. **B**, **C**, **E** and **F**.

NAPLAN-style Conventions of Language Test 1 PAGE 31

1. fraudulent
2. centuries
3. elixir
4. concentration
5. headache
6. absolutely
7. **B**.
8. **B**.
9. **A**.
10. e.g. fraudulent, fake, non-existent
11. tug; send
12. **C**.
13. **C**.
14. A scammer is someone who pretends to have skills or knowledge
15. **C**.
16. **A**.

Unit 8A PAGE 32

1. **C**. See lines 12–13.
2. **C**; **B**. See lines 2–3 and 6–7.
3. **C**. You can infer that he coos to soothe and reassure them, i.e. that he can be trusted.
4. **A**, **B**, **C** and **D**.
5. **H**. You should judge that a story with the title 'The magic lamp' is likely to be fantasy. You might also judge that the story is a mystery (**G**) or an adventure (**A**) if the children have to find their father.
6. Responses will vary. You could judge that Asifa is older because she manages the phone with the map and Dad had messaged her and not Tariq. You could judge that Tariq is older because he seems responsible for the money and he tells Asifa not to touch anything. Also Dad might have messaged Asifa rather than Tariq because she is the youngest and might worry more than Tariq.

Unit 8B PAGE 33

1. crowded
2. muted
3. quieter
4. unlucky: not lucky/unfortunate
5. Suggested answers: breakage, breaking, broke, break, broken
6. from the French, Arabic and Persian *bazar* meaning marketplace
7. **C**.
8. **C**.
9. people who sell food or other goods from a stall on the street or in a market
10. **B**.
11. **A**.
12. the map on her phone
13. **A** was situated; was kept
    B kept
14. e.g. into the shop
15. e.g. until we find Dad, while we look for Dad
16. **A**.
17. 'This is where Dad was,' said Asifa.
18. 'If we can find Dad, we'll be alright,' said Tariq.

Unit 8C PAGE 34

1. **B**.
2. **A**.
3. Everything begged to be touched.

ANSWERS

4. C.
5. A, C and D. B is incorrect because readers know why the children are in the bazaar.
6. A, B, C, D, E, F and G.
7. Responses will vary.

Unit 9A PAGE 35

1. B. See lines 2–4 and 8.
2. C. See lines 6–10 and 15–16.
3. C. You can infer that C is correct because the text states that 'Anne was good with computer coding but Erik wasn't'.
4. A, C and D.
5. A, B and D.
6. A, B and C.

Unit 9B PAGE 36

1. appreciated
2. exciting
3. encountered
4. disconnected: not connected, unlinked
5. Suggested answers: excited, excitement, excitedly, excitable
6. from the Latin *communitas* meaning the feeling of togetherness
7. C.
8. D.
9. the sequence of events in a story (narrative)
10. C.
11. D.
12. an exciting moment
13. A chose; was
    B was
14. e.g. for weeks
15. e.g. they had written/that they liked
16. B.
17. Erik and Anne made a good team.
18. The free program was called Twine.

Unit 9C PAGE 37

1. B.
2. D.
3. third person, Erik
4. D.
5. Erik and Anne are likely to enjoy playing computer games and might be interested in this site to find games to play as well as to get ideas for their own game.
6. Responses will vary.
7. Responses will vary.

Unit 10A PAGE 38

1. D. See lines 6–8 and 19–21.
2. B. See line 2.
3. A, B and C.
4. 1 The characters are pretty much stereotypes based on gender and good versus evil.
   2 The moral themes (treating animals as assets, experimenting with DNA and getting something scientists couldn't have imagined, animal welfare issues) will be lost on most viewers.
5. You can judge that tension is important in an action movie to create excitement and suspense and to keep viewers wondering what will happen next.
6. A, B and D.

Unit 10B PAGE 39

1. special
2. protagonist
3. stereotyped
4. imperfect: not perfect
5. Suggested answers: acknowledge, acknowledged, unacknowledged
6. from the 1960s Disney term meaning the creation of lifelike robots
7. A.
8. B.
9. deoxyribonucleic acid: the gene code of a living thing that determines all its characteristics
10. C.
11. B.
12. *Jurassic World*
13. A Using; is; suffer
    B is; suffer
14. e.g. in modern times
15. e.g. because it had great action sequences
16. C.
17. 'It's an exciting film,' said Nadia.
18. Nadia doesn't agree with the exploitation of animals.

Unit 10C PAGE 40

1. C.
2. B. The text ends with a call to action.
3. Suggested answers: exciting, tense, fantastic, amazing, spectacular
4. Suggested answers: inspire, fantastic, enrichment, stimulated, wonderful, confined, sad
5. The inset box defines zoochosis, which is a mental disease affecting animals confined in the worst types of zoos described by the author.
6. The authors of both texts discuss animals in captivity. Text 1 gives an opinion that animals in a theme park are being used for entertainment. Text 2 gives an opinion that, while zoos are places people go to for entertainment, their primary role is for education. The author of Text 1 expresses concern about animal welfare in an imaginary theme park. The author of Text 2 expresses an opinion about the differences in the welfare of animals between the best zoos and the worst zoos.
7. Responses will vary.

ANSWERS

Unit 11A PAGE 41

1. **A**, **B** and **C**. See lines 8–13.
2. **C**. See lines 10–13.
3. Responses will vary. Suggested answers:
   - trying to keep people physically active
   - trying to get people to continue their hobbies
   - trying to keep people engaged with others
   - trying to get people to go to the dining room for meals and interaction
   - trying to get people to join in the sing-a-longs
4. Grandpa basically now lives in one room in aged care. You can infer that he moved from his own home, which would have been larger than one room. His world has also shrunk because it seems he rarely leaves the aged-care facility to go anywhere. He certainly does not go out on his own as he relies on others to take him out.
5. **D**. It's likely Grandpa is sad but it's also likely he is hopeful that he will adjust and get used to his new home. His family thinks so and is supportive.
6. You can judge that Nellie hopes Grandpa settles in, makes friends, joins in with some of the activities and adjusts to his new home.

Unit 11B PAGE 42

1. residential
2. conversations
3. Adjusting
4. discourage: try to prevent someone from doing something
5. Suggested answers: connect, connection, connected, connecting, disconnect, disconnected, disconnecting, reconnect, reconnecting, reconnection
6. DJ stands for disc jockey, a term coined in 1945 in the USA for someone who played records (discs) on the radio.
7. **C**.
8. **C**.
9. a network of friends, family and other personal contacts
10. **D**.
11. **A**.
12. he's shrinking
13. **A** enjoyed, settled, was
    B settled, was
14. e.g. into aged care
15. e.g. Grandpa has shrunk, Grandpa is getting smaller and shorter
16. **B**.
17. 'How is the food?' asked Mum.
18. 'It's not too bad but I'd prefer to cook my own,' said Grandpa.

Unit 11C PAGE 43

1. **B**.
2. **C** and **E**.
3. Kim. Kim's comments are very definite. Kim uses high modality words such as 'Knitting is', 'can't just decide' and 'That doesn't make sense'. Rola uses low modality: 'could be', 'probably can be', 'I think', 'maybe'. Hamish uses low modality: 'probably can't be'. Carl uses low modality: 'Some people might think'.
4. Rola supports her opinions with evidence or arguments.
5. The expression 'ants in your pants' means you are always active and moving and can't sit still, like you have ants in your pants and they are annoying you and you are trying to shake them out.
6. Text 1 mentions the importance of hobbies for health and wellbeing. Text 2 discusses different hobbies the children or their family members have.
7. Responses will vary.

Unit 12A PAGE 44

1. **D**. See lines 9–10.
2. **B**. See lines 5–6.
3. **A**. Bonney must have been courageous and determined to have achieved what she did. You can't infer that Bonney was timid or outspoken. She was likely intelligent but the best answer is **A**.
4. A pioneer is the first person to do something. These pilots all achieved 'firsts' and broke aviation records.
5. You should judge that the Australian military was sexist at that time and, in spite of her many achievements, Bonney was not accepted because she was female.
6. You would likely feel outraged, annoyed, angry and insulted because it was so unfair but you would also be a product of the times and understand that it would be impossible to fight the military and win the right to join as a pilot or trainer and so, just like Bonney did, you likely would have given up.

Unit 12B PAGE 45

1. circumnavigated
2. meritorious
3. Angel
4. unlicensed (adjective): without a licence, unauthorised
5. Suggested answers: reversed, reversing, reversible, irreversible
6. AM: Member of the Order of Australia (340 AMs are awarded each year. The Award was established in 1975 by Prime Minister Gough Whitlam and Queen Elizabeth II.)

MBE: Member of the Order of the British Empire (an award established in 1917 by King George)

7. **D.**

8. **B.**

9. the usual wind direction for a place or season

10. **D.**

11. **A.**

12. an elite group: aviators

13. **A** Flying; was; broke
B broke

14. e.g. from England

15. was given, qualified; who was given her first flying lesson by Charles Kingsford Smith

16. **C.**

17. Bonney was the first woman to fly from Australia to South Africa.

18. Bert Hinkler was from Bundaberg, Queensland.

Unit 12C PAGE 46

1. to inform; to provide information about women's voting rights

2. Year 6 students should understand the terms used in the text except perhaps for suffrage, which is defined in the text in lines 15–16.

3. Bold is used for the dates which are the milestones referred to in the title of the text. The name Catherine Helen Spence is in bold because she achieved a milestone in her political career.

4. In her speech Spence hopes she has achieved things that make the world a better place for all. She feels that it is her responsibility to use her wisdom and abilities ('capacity') for the benefit of the wider world and not just for her own family.

5. It seems that Spence was intelligent, outspoken, courageous and determined. You might also think she was brave because she had to stand up for women's rights at a time when doing so would not have been easy.

6. Both texts describe strong women who had successful careers in fields dominated by men at that time.

7. Responses will vary.

Unit 13A PAGE 47

1. **B**. See lines 3–4.

2. acidic; too acidic for coral to survive. (See lines 7–8.)

3. **A**, **B**, **D**, **F** and **G**.

4. **A**, **C** and **D**

5. **C.**

6. all ocean coral will die

Unit 13B PAGE 48

1. Amphibians

2. Pollutants

3. emissions

4. undamaged: have no damage

5. Suggested answers: reduced, reducing, reduction, reducible

6. from the Latin *spec(ere)* meaning look or regard; the noun species relates to appearance or form

7. **D.**

8. **A.**

9. long-term change in the earth's climate due to increasing carbon dioxide in the atmosphere, largely created through the burning of fossil fuels

10. **B.**

11. **A.**

12. the oceans

13. **A** Prevent; is
B is

14. permanently, completely

15. e.g. coral cannot survive

16. **A.**

17. The Great Barrier Reef is under threat.

18. 'Storms, sediment, pollution and carbon dioxide hurt the GBR,' said Sacher.

Unit 13C PAGE 49

1. Text 1: to persuade
Text 2: to inform

2. museumgoers in the future (some time after 2030)

3. that many animals will become extinct in the future and/or that the rate of extinctions increases rapidly after 2007 from 457 to 97 745

4. extinctions, captivity, survive, abandon, drowning, entangled, butchering

5. The prediction of Text 1 has come true in Text 2.
or
Text 1 warns that unless something is done to limit climate change, the only way to see coral in the future will be in a museum. Text 2 is a museum exhibit in the future, which features coral bred in captivity.

6. **C** and **D**.

7. Responses will vary.

Unit 14A PAGE 50

1. **A**, **B** and **D**. See lines 9–10.

2. **B**, **C**, **D** and **E**. See lines 12–13.

3. **C.**

4. **A.** (**B** is also likely.)

5. **A**, **B**, **D** and **E**.

6. Suggested answers: 1 Liam has been fortunate because his aunt has a rock-climbing gym where he can practise for free. 2 His aunt is a competitive rock climber who introduced Liam to the sport and who obviously supports Liam's interest. 3 His sister loves the sport too so they can do it together. 4 Because he loves it he is happy to put in time and effort, which helps him improve. 5 The better you are at something, the more

ANSWERS

you enjoy it and the happier you are to spend more time improving.

Unit 14B PAGE 51

1. competitive
2. safety
3. physically
4. incorrect: wrong/not correct
5. Suggested answers: flexing, inflexible, flexibly, flexibility, flexibleness
6. from the German *abseilen* (*ab*—down + *seilen*—to rope) meaning rope down
7. **D**.
8. **C**.
9. not natural; made by humans
10. **C**.
11. **D**.
12. rock climbing
13. **A** climb; is
    B is
14. well, regularly
15. owns, get to train; so we get to train there for free
16. **C**.
17. You need to be fit, flexible and strong.
18. 'Our aunt's gym is fantastic!' exclaimed Liam.

Unit 14C PAGE 52

1. Text 1: first person
   Text 2: second person
2. **A** and **B**.
3. Yes it does. The text states that the oldest current member is 86 but you can infer that anyone older could become a member of the club and cycle if they wanted to as the text says 'All welcome'.
4. **B**, **C** and **D**.
5. **A**, **B**, **C** and **D**.
6. **A**, **B**, **C** and **F**.
7. Responses will vary.

Unit 15A PAGE 53

1. **A**, **B**, **C** and **D**. See line 12.
2. Mum and Dad liked a movie with that title. (See line 9.)
3. **A**, **B**, **C** and **D**.
4. **A**, **C** and **D**. You can infer that Dad does these tasks because these don't involve cramped spaces under houses or working at height.
5. Suggested answers: 1 The writer sounds proud of Mum and Dad and can speak knowledgeably about the business. 2 Mum and Dad take pride in their work and their business and they like their work. 3 They look happy in the photo. 4 They likely get customers who want to have a female plumber visit their home.
6. **A**, **B** and **D**. You can judge that the writer is proud of Mum and Dad. You can tell that the parents have a sense of humour because of the name they chose for their business. Dad would value having a female plumber in the business for the extra clients it might attract. **C** is incorrect because the writer has free choice and can make the decision to join the family business for herself. **E** is incorrect because you can tell that Dad is happy and proud to work with a female plumber.

Unit 15B PAGE 54

1. plumbers
2. apprenticeships
3. business
4. undecided: not having reached a decision
5. Suggested answers: custom, customs, customary, customarily
6. an initialism for polyvinyl chloride, a type of rigid plastic developed around 1930
7. **B**.
8. **A**.
9. a system of working while training for a trade
10. **D**.
11. **B**.
12. copper
13. **A** renovating; is; enjoy
    B is; enjoy
14. when they were studying
15. who don't look anything like my parents
16. **A**.
17. 'Dad's surname is Thomsen,' said Jayda.
18. 'Mum's happy to work on the roof,' declared Jayda.

Unit 15C PAGE 55

1. discrimination against people with hearing loss
2. a braille computer
3. discrimination based on gender and disability (hearing, vision)
4. Responses will vary. The AA would be very happy that they employed Douglas. He has been a loyal employee for 17 years and is very good at his job. Based on research he likely would have had fewer days off work and fewer safety incidents than people without disability.
5. argues; unfairly
6. Responses will vary. If Douglas could not get a job because of his disability he would have been unemployed for the last 17 years. This would have had a negative impact on his self-esteem and feelings of self-worth. He would have had a lower standard of living and would have been financially dependent on others.
7. Responses will vary.

NAPLAN-style Reading Test 2 PAGES 56–57

1. **D**.
2. **B**.
3. **D**.

4. C.
5. B.
6. C.
7. The heading of Text 1 is effective. A vessel has landed. It is presumed that aliens are onboard because the text talks of war. No-one knows where the vessel came from or what's inside. The job of a headline is to make people want to read the article. This headline will grab the reader's attention. The heading of Text 2 is not effective. It is boring.
8. **A** (her face a blank page), **B**, **C**, **D** and **G** (looks like an army camp).
9. **A**, **B** and **C**.
10. **B**.
11. **A**, **D**, **E** and **F**.
12. **A**, **D** and **E** are the best answers. Erin seems brave and independent (**A** and **D**) because she stands up to Doreen and is about to test a mystery gadget on her own. **E** is also correct because you could judge that she is curious about the gadget and about where her mother and grandfather have gone. **B** and **C** could also be true but are not the best answers. You might judge that Erin is foolish and reckless for testing a mysterious gadget on her own and for wilfully annoying Doreen to the point where she would 'cop it later' but Erin trusts her grandfather and so trusts she can use the gadget he has left for her.

NAPLAN-style Conventions of Language Test 2 PAGE 58

1. personnel
2. Field
3. aliens
4. occupants
5. mysterious
6. Furniture
7. **D**.
8. **A**.
9. **B**.
10. **C**.
11. had vanished
12. **D**.
13. **B**.
14. until we can confirm that it's safe
15. **B**.
16. **D**.

Unit 16A PAGE 59

1. **D**. See lines 3–5.
2. **B**. See line 8.
3. **B**.
4. **D**.
5. **C**.
6. **A**, **B** and **C**.

Unit 16B PAGE 60

1. grapevine
2. doesn't
3. frugal
4. disloyal: not loyal
5. Suggested answers: scientific, scientifically, unscientific, unscientifically
6. grape + vine, first used in the American civil war to imply a rumour
7. **C**.
8. **A**.
9. aerospace engineering; engineering for space
10. **D**.
11. **B**.
12. You're saving for a bike.
13. Nan had been thinking about bicycles, Nan was thinking about bicycles
14. is, need; whenever you need grandmothering
15. when
16. **B**.
17. Although you've been given $10, you shouldn't spend it.
18. In the morning, after breakfast, I'll go to the bank.

Unit 16C PAGE 61

1. **B**.
2. **C**.
3. **A** and **D**.
4. You can infer that Dr Scott was a respected Australian who campaigned for Indigenous rights, land rights, civil rights and environmental protections.
5. **A** and **C**.
6. You should judge that the grandmother would feel proud of what has been written. The words show that the narrator loves and respects the grandmother and values her opinion.
7. Responses will vary.

Unit 17A PAGE 62

1. **C**. See lines 3 and 22–23.
2. a strategy used by writers to provide information to the reader about something that happened in the past (See lines 9–10.)
3. **B**.
4. the indigenous people of the Alaskan tundra/North Slope of Alaska
5. **D**.
6. Answers will vary.

Unit 17B PAGE 63

1. language
2. observation
3. behaviour
4. irrelevant: not relevant, not related or important
5. Suggested answers: knowledgeable, acknowledge, acknowledging, acknowledged, acknowledgement
6. from the French *toundra* and the Russian *tundra*, which

came from the Sami *tundar* meaning flat mountain area

7. **D.**
8. **C.**
9. a character in a literary text who develops, grows and changes in personality or attitude
10. **A.**
11. **D.**
12. **B.**
13. In the story, Miyax makes dangerous mistakes.
14. runs, has been, becomes; although she has been out on the tundra before
15. although
16. **B.**
17. Although Miyax's interaction with the wolves is fascinating, it's a sad story.
18. *Julie of the Wolves* was written by Jean Craighead George.

Unit 17C PAGE 64

1. **D.**
2. **C.**
3. give an opinion about hunting and about using animals for sport and entertainment
4. It alerts people that the next bit of the review gives away an important part of the plot and so might spoil their enjoyment of the story.
5. a theme in *Julie of the Wolves*, the book reviewed in Text 1, is that hunting animals for sport is wrong. This is the theme of Text 2.
6. **A**, **B**, **C**, **D** and **E.**
7. Responses will vary.

Unit 18A PAGE 65

1. paramedic (See line 2.)
2. in his and Elaine's own backyard (See lines 18–19.)
3. **A**, **B**, **C**, **E**, **F**, **G** and **H.**
4. Responses will vary. Uncle Ronnie likely felt that libraries are important places for everyone in the community to use and enjoy. Libraries offer free use of books and other materials. Uncle Ronnie might have worried that people would have to travel too far to get to another library and that might stop people from reading or learning. He may also be a keen reader who would miss the library.
5. **B**. You can infer that the most important reason Scarlet admires Ronnie is the first one mentioned in her text. She devotes two paragraphs to Ronnie's job.
6. Responses will vary. You can judge that Ronnie believes people need to become activists and protest for change if they feel strongly about something. He might also mean that people can be counted when they vote for political candidates who promise to change things in ways that they agree with.

Unit 18B PAGE 66

1. paramedic
2. Ambulance
3. library
4. uninvolved: not involved/disinterested/distant
5. Suggested answers: attend, attendance, attending, attendant
6. from the 1950s military term for a medical worker who parachuted into an emergency situation: para(chute) + medic
7. **C.**
8. **A.**
9. a person who campaigns for social or political change
10. **B.**
11. **A.**
12. **C.**
13. Ronnie is/has been nominated for a citizenship award.
14. believes, is close; when an issue is close to his heart
15. when
16. **B.**
17. Ronnie's wedding was in the backyard.
18. Ronnie and Elaine were married in February 2023.

Unit 18C PAGE 67

1. **D.**
2. **C.**
3. **B**, **D**, **E** and **F.**
4. the 'need' to do something about cleaning up the rubbish—especially plastic rubbish—on the beaches
5. **D.**
6. Both texts feature people admired for their activism and volunteer work in the local community.
7. Responses will vary.

Unit 19A PAGE 68

1. Gorm, in the neighbouring kingdom (See lines 15–17.)
2. **C**. See line 9.
3. the Magus.
4. **B**, **C**, **E** and **F.**
5. **C.**
6. **C.**

Unit 19B PAGE 69

1. anticipated
2. impatient
3. guards
4. undisturbed: not disturbed, not moved
5. Suggested answers: neighbour, neighbourly, neighbourhood
6. a Latin word from the Greek *mangos* and the old Persian *magys* meaning magician or sorcerer
7. **C.**

ANSWERS

8. **B.**
9. acting without thinking and without proper consideration of the consequences of the action
10. **B.**
11. **A.**
12. **D.**
13. Helga is looking/looks at the door.
14. for their lives depended on it
15. because
16. **C.**
17. Helga would prefer to go to Gorm.
18. The chapter's title is 'Seeking the Magus'.

Unit 19C PAGE 70

1. to find (seek out) the Magus
2. **C.**
3. the main character in a story
4. **C.**
5. the setting in the illustration, the characters of the Queen's Guard and the Magus (a sorcerer/magician), a kingdom called Gorm
6. pirates, fairies, water sprites and dragons, in fantastical settings, magic and spells
7. Responses will vary.

Unit 20A PAGE 71

1. Australia (See line 23.)
2. desert (See lines 7–9.)
3. **C.**
4. Increasing the migration corridor helps the animals complete a successful migration and supports conservation efforts. Conserving animals and their habitats ensures that the tour company will have a tourist attraction in the future.
5. If the local people value tourism they will see that it's in their interest to look after the things the tourists come to see, such as the wild animals and the natural environment. This means that instead of killing the animals for food, or because they plunder their crops, people will value the live animals.
6. Responses will vary. The grandparents describe complex situations and use sophisticated terminology. They obviously respect Matilda's ability to read and comprehend this information and they think that she is interested in it. They respect her level of thinking and capacity to understand complex concepts. They don't talk down to her. They seem keen to expand her knowledge about the world and teach her things. They declare their love for her. It seems a warm and loving relationship.

Unit 20B PAGE 72

1. philosophy
2. Desert
3. highlands
4. undervalued: not valued enough
5. Suggested answers: communicate, communicable, communicated, communicating, communicative, uncommunicative
6. from the Latin *indigena* meaning native; indigenous with a lowercase 'i' refers to native or First Nation people in countries other than Australia
7. **B.**
8. **D.**
9. the language used by the government, in the courts and in schools
10. **D.**
11. **B.**
12. **C.**
13. The company funds/is funding the two housing projects.
14. when we get back
15. therefore
16. **C.**
17. 'UNESCO does a good job,' said Ted.
18. 'We're enjoying the tour of Botswana,' said Nana.

Unit 20C PAGE 73

1. **A**, **B** and **C.**
2. **D.**
3. **B.**
4. **B.**
5. **A**, **B** and **C.** There is evidence in both texts to support these judgements. **D** is incorrect. You can judge that Matilda's grandparents are interested in human-rights issues such as health and education but there's nothing in either text to show that Matilda's mother is.
6. Responses will vary. You need to read each text and draw conclusions about Matilda's family relationships, behaviour and attitude in order to compare them with your own. Suggested answers:
   - My family likes to travel but no-one has been overseas. My family likes to travel around Australia. Like Matilda's family, my family likes to have holidays in areas of natural beauty.
   - Matilda lives in a single-parent household. I do too but I live with my father.
   - My grandparents use the internet all the time to post photos just like Matilda's grandparents do.
   - My relationship with my grandparents is nothing like Matilda's with hers. I don't have anything to do with my grandparents. I rarely communicate with them. They don't know how to use the internet or post photos online.
7. Responses will vary.

Unit 21A PAGE 74

1. 1 Elephants range across vast areas of countryside.
   2 Poachers use drones and other high-tech equipment to track elephants and avoid rangers.
   (See lines 7–9.)
2. They destroy it. (See lines 10–11.)
3. **A**, **B**, **D**, **E** and **F**.
4. **C**, **D**, **E** and **F**.
5. **B** and **D**.

Unit 21B PAGE 75

1. rhinoceros
2. hippopotamus
3. orphaned
4. unprotected: not protected
5. Suggested answers: destroyed, destroying, destruction, destructive, destructively, destructible, indestructible
6. from the Latin past participle *confiscatus* meaning put away in a chest, it now means declare something the property of the Treasury (government); lawfully seize or take property
7. **B**.
8. **C**.
9. a person with the job of taking care of wildlife and the environment
10. **A**.
11. **C**.
12. **C**.
13. Elephants are killed by poachers, Poachers kill elephants
14. after we'd pitched the tent
15. consequently
16. **A**.
17. Babies witnessed their mothers' deaths.
18. If people understood poaching, they wouldn't buy ivory.

Unit 21C PAGE 76

1. the Convention on International Trade in Endangered Species of Wild Fauna and Flora
2. 1 their body parts
   2 to stop them circling over dead elephants
3. Text 1: **C** and **D**.
   Text 2: **C** and **E**.
4. The agreement is an attempt to protect animals from extinction but it is not always successful. It's meant to do a job but it doesn't or can't.
5. The aim is to use emotive language to make people feel bad about the hurt caused by ivory. People who buy it might not realise the pain and suffering caused to get the ivory, or the threat of elephant extinction.
6. Vulture body parts are used in traditional medicines because some people mistakenly believe that vultures have magical powers.
7. Responses will vary.

Unit 22A PAGE 77

1. The children fight and get sent outside. They receive gifts that only please them for a short time and then they want something new. (See lines 10–17.)
2. human greed, waste, people starving, fallow (unfertile) ground, deforestation, pollution, landfill, plastic in the ocean, Christmas trees and decorations being unsustainable (See lines 18–39.)
3. **D**.
4. **D**.
5. **B**.
6. **A**, **B**, **C**, **D** and **F**.

Unit 22B PAGE 78

1. receiving
2. squabbling
3. outrageous
4. dissatisfaction: not being satisfied
5. Suggested answers: volunteered, volunteering, voluntary, voluntarily
6. from the Old English *Cristes maesse* meaning Christ's mass
7. **A**.
8. **B**.
9. the period of time around Christmas and New Year when there are festivities and celebrations
10. **B**.
11. **B**.
12. **C**.
13. Those in need get/are getting help from the family, The family helps/is helping those in need
14. While I used to love decorations
15. My mum, who volunteers for Landcare, gives her time to help the environment.
16. **C**.
17. We're giving things that we don't need.
18. WWF stands for World Wildlife Fund.

Unit 22C PAGE 79

1. **D**.
2. **C**.
3. all things that end up being thrown into landfill, such as plastic plates and forks, Christmas trees and decorations
4. You should judge that shops sell things people want to buy. If people stopped buying items then shops would not stock them so manufacturers would

stop making them. Ultimately the choices consumers make impact on what is sold in stores. Governments can also stop items from being sold if the items are toxic or dangerous.

5. C.
6. C.
7. Responses will vary.

Unit 23A PAGE 80

1. for national pride and to encourage people to get fitter and healthier (See lines 2–6.)
2. **A**, **B**, **C** and **D**. See lines 17–18.
3. **D**.
4. **C**.
5. government funding or grants, family support, jobs, prize money, product endorsements, sponsorship
6. **C**.

Unit 23B PAGE 81

1. subsidise
2. Paralympics
3. outweighed
4. international: between countries/nations
5. Suggested answers: subsidy, subsidising, subsidised, subsidisation
6. from the ancient Greek *Olympikos* meaning Olympus or Olympia: Olympus is a mountain in Greece and the mythical abode of the Greek Gods. The Olympics is a modern revival of the ancient games that began in Greece in 1896. (Ancient games were staged in Olympia in Greece from 776 BC to 393 AD.)
7. **D**.
8. **C**.
9. the action of supporting something
10. **B**.
11. **A**.
12. **B**.
13. Athletes win prize money.
14. Whenever I watch the Paralympics
15. Whenever
16. **C**.
17. Clothing, food, watches and vehicles are products that athletes endorse.
18. The government's grants to athletes are being questioned.

Unit 23C PAGE 82

1. **E**.
2. **A**, **C** and **D**.
3. **A**, **B**, **C**, **D**, **F**, **H**, **I**, **K**, **L** and **M**.
4. The athlete's reputation would likely be damaged. The brand's reputation could be damaged. Consumers might be disappointed and disillusioned. They might not like to use that particular product or brand anymore.
5. Text 1 mentions endorsements while Text 2 is an example of an endorsement.
6. To get an endorsement deal the athlete needs to be famous and popular so that people will want what they endorse. It's important to associate a brand with a top performance because the athlete's fame helps promote the product. The athlete's image rubs off on the product and influences people who look up to the athlete or want to be like them.
7. Responses will vary.

NAPLAN-style Reading Test 3 PAGES 83–84

1. **D**.
2. **A**.
3. **A**.
4. **D**.
5. **A**.
6. **C**, **D** and **E**.
7. Alice thinks the story is meant to put her to sleep but Grandfather tells her that storytellers prefer to keep their audience awake by telling interesting or exciting stories rather than boring ones.
8. third; first
9. **A**.
10. **A**, **C** and **E**.
11. gladsome voice; heart leapt with joy
12. Grandfather will tell a story about the chair and Alice will fall asleep.

NAPLAN-style Conventions of Language Test 3 PAGE 85

1. pleasant
2. decayed
3. curiously
4. Foliage
5. trundled
6. likeness
7. **D**.
8. **C**.
9. **A**.
10. The chair
11. had been
12. **C**.
13. **A**.
14. which had a savage grin
15. **C**.
16. **B**.

Unit 24A PAGE 86

1. Toad, the girl and the girl's aunt (the washerwoman)
2. a cell or room in a castle prison
3. He is imprisoned and wants to escape.
4. Toad is the main obstacle to his escape from prison. He is not a good listener and seems too vain to listen to advice. He also appears to be too vain to want

to dress as a washerwoman in order to escape.

5. **A**, **B**, **D**, **E** and **I**
6. Toad says 'There, there,' and makes a joke, implying that he thinks the girl is embarrassed to admit that her aunt is a cleaner. He is patronising. Toad thinks washerwomen/cleaners are lowly and inferior to him. He makes a disparaging joke that his own aunts ought to be washerwomen. It seems he does not like his aunts and thinks lowly jobs like washerwomen would suit their characters.

Unit 24B PAGE 87

1. arrangement
2. official
3. ungrateful
4. indifference: disinterest, lack of concern
5. Suggested answers: escape, escaping, escapee, escapade
6. a carriage pulled by four horses; carriages used to be made in the 15th century in a Hungarian town called Kocs and so they were called 'carriage of Kocs' or coach
7. **A**.
8. **C**.
9. physical appearance or body shape (It is likely Toad and the aunt have big stomachs.)
10. **C**.
11. **B**.
12. an aunt who is a washerwoman
13. might
14. e.g. definitely, certainly, absolutely
15. e.g. Although
16. **C**.
17. You'll need to be quiet,' said the girl.
18. The girl said, 'Don't be so annoying.'

Unit 24C PAGE 88

1. Both Text 1 and Text 2 seem to be advocating having positive thoughts, gratitude and kindness to others. They each seem to have a lesson to teach about how we relate to others. Text 1 tells how Toad's attitude prevents him from seeing the girl as helpful or kind. Text 2 describes how the children's disagreeable thoughts and attitudes impact on their health and wellbeing.
2. Responses will vary. Based on the language and grammar of the texts and the way they are written, readers would likely have needed to be competent at reading and comprehension.
3. Suggested answers: Mistress Mary, moorland cottages, common little Yorkshire housemaids, moor boy
4. The girl in the first paragraph, Mistress Mary, did not like anyone and was determined to be disagreeable until nature (the robins, springtime, the gardens) started to occupy her thoughts and take over from the nasty thoughts.

   In the second paragraph the boy Colin chooses to stay hidden in his room all day, focusing on his own weaknesses and his dislike of himself and of people looking at him. However, he begins to change by being open to sunshine and beauty and becoming more courageous.
5. It means that if you occupy yourself with good, kind deeds and think beautiful thoughts there's no room to dwell on prickly, ugly or disagreeable thoughts. Your mind will be too focused on beauty to have any time for nastiness and beauty will grow in you if you tend it like a garden.
6. Responses will vary. You can infer that Text 1 is about an animal named Toad who is very rich and thinks he is superior to everyone else. Text 2 is about a girl called Mistress Mary and a boy named Colin. Your choice could be based on whether you like stories about talking animals or whether you think the adventures of Mistress Mary and Colin sound more interesting.
7. Responses will vary.

Unit 25A PAGE 89

1. Student Action for Aborigines (See line 2.)
2. **D**. See lines 13–14.
3. **B**.
4. **A**, **C** and **D**.
5. **C**.
6. **A**, **B**, **E** and **F**.

Unit 25B PAGE 90

1. racial
2. Segregationist
3. university
4. mistreatment/maltreatment/ill-treatment: treat badly
5. Suggested answers: investigated, investigating, investigation, investigator, investigative
6. from the Latin *indigena* meaning native; Indigenous with a capital 'I' refers specifically to First Nation Australian peoples
7. **C**.
8. **D**.
9. a written law
10. **B**.
11. **C**.
12. American events that highlighted discrimination
13. must
14. e.g. overwhelmingly, certainly, really

15. but
16. **B**.
17. The group visited Dubbo, Walgett, Moree, Tenterfield, Grafton, Lismore and Kempsey.
18. Students from Sydney University formed SAFA (Student Action for Aborigines).

Unit 25C PAGE 91

1. **B** and **C**.
2. **D**.
3. **A**.
4. **A**, **B** and **C**. (Note that **D** is a human right and is not specific to First Nation Australians as the original peoples).
5. They both deal with issues of human and civil rights. They both feature stamps showing First Nation Australians who were civil-rights activists.
6.

Human rights
to live freely to be treated fairly to live in safety to live without fear of persecution, torture or detainment to have adequate food, water, medicine and shelter to have an education to have a family
Civil rights
fair pay for work the right to a fair trial a free press the right to vote
Social justice
everyone gets the same access to clean running water, sanitation, education, employment, housing and health care

7. Responses will vary.

Unit 26A PAGE 92

1. **B**. See lines 9–10.
2. **C**. See lines 11–12.
3. **A**, **B**, **C** and **E**.
4. **D**.
5. **A**. You can judge that the host is neutral. The host's role is to ask questions and to clarify for viewers what the guest speaker is saying. The only view expressed by the host is that they 'hadn't thought of soil in that way'. This comment does not make any judgement about the ideas themselves; it simply shows that the ideas are new to the host.
6. A pun is wordplay that relies on different meanings of the same word. The expression 'food for thought' means that ideas are food for the brain, i.e. new ideas stimulate the brain and nourish it. Thomas talks about feeding the soil and it in turn feeding us. The pun is in the different use of the concept of food: food we eat, food for our brains and food for the soil.

Unit 26B PAGE 93

1. deforestation
2. actively
3. fertilisers
4. inability/disability: lack of ability
5. Suggested answers: excited, excitable, excitedly, excitability
6. chemicals used to kill insects; first used in 1939 as a combination of the English word pest and the Latin suffix *-cide* meaning killer
7. **C**.
8. **D**.
9. a personal financial interest
10. **B**.
11. **B**.
12. what is being done to the soil all over the world in the name of food
13. must
14. e.g. definitely, certainly, absolutely
15. e.g. Because, As, Since
16. **B**.
17. It's important that soil maintains its quality.
18. 'The soil's ability to regenerate is amazing,' said Thomas.

Unit 26C PAGE 94

1. **C**.
2. **D**.
3. treated sewage from people's homes
4. Text 1: **D** and **F**.
   Text 2: **B**, **C** and **E**.
5. Text 1 tells of the importance of soil regeneration. Text 2 tells of the use of biosolids to regenerate soil.
6. **B**.
7. Responses will vary.

Unit 27A PAGE 95

1. adding strange ingredients to a cauldron to make a magic potion (See lines 6 and 12–19.)
2. the forked tongue of a kind of snake—the death adder (See line 16.)
3. **C**.
4. Hecate seems to be in charge. She congratulates (commends) the witches and tells them they will share in the benefits of the spell (th' gains).
5. casting a spell on the ingredients so that they work for the witches
6. It is scary and spooky. The setting is a cave so it must be dark and the only light is from the fire where the giant pot is bubbling. There are three

witches and Hecate, and the sound of thunder so a storm is raging outside the cave. The witches mention horrible-sounding ingredients. The fire burns and the witches seem to be evil.

Unit 27B PAGE 96

1. Adder's
2. blind-worm's
3. tongue
4. untroubled: not troubled or bothered
5. Suggested answers: powered, powering, powerful, powerless, powerfully, powerlessly
6. from the Latin *caldaria* and the Middle English *cauderon* meaning large pot for boiling
7. D.
8. A.
9. a large cave
10. C.
11. B.
12. the lizard's leg that had been chewed on by the cat
13. shall
14. e.g. definitely, certainly, absolutely
15. e.g. Because, As, Since
16. C.
17. 'Well done!' declared Hecate.
18. 'It's a blindworm's sting,' said Second Witch.

Unit 27C PAGE 97

1. snakes
2. Well done! I admire your efforts, and every one of you will share in the rewards.
3. Suggested answers:

   Assonance: trouble—bubble; aware—hair; petrify—eye

   Simile: like a hell-broth; like elves and fairies in a ring

   Rhyme: snake—bake; frog—dog; sting—wing; double—trouble—bubble; pains—gains; sing—ring; hair—despair; distress—dress; toil—coil; Band—stand; spit—it; aware—hair

   Alliteration: fillet—fenny; boil—bake; Lizard's leg; separate—stand—sway—spit
4. The snakes did not like music. They would 'stand On end and sway and writhe and spit' and Medusa's hair would turn back into a disaster.
5. 'And, being woman and aware Of such disaster to her hair'

   Women were judged as superficial and overly concerned with appearances. The poem says Medusa petrified anyone she met. To be petrified means to be frozen in fear and unable to move. In Greek mythology the Medusa turned people to stone if they looked at her. A synonym for petrify is fossilise: where organic matter is turned to a stony substance over time.
6. Both texts use a rhyme pattern (rhyming couplets). They were both written a long time ago. They were both written by men and are about evil women: Medusa and witches. The women are scary and inflict harm.
7. Responses will vary.

Unit 28A PAGE 98

1. B. See lines 9–10.
2. Its last speakers die. (See line 11.)
3. C.
4. C.
5. B, C and E.
6. B, C and D.

Unit 28B PAGE 99

1. Indigenous
2. critically
3. scientific
4. invaluable: very valuable, of high value, priceless
5. culture, cultured, culturally
6. from the Latin *communitas* meaning the public
7. A.
8. D.
9. when a person or group feels insignificant or unimportant
10. C.
11. B.
12. which means flesh-eating
13. might
14. possibly
15. e.g. Meanwhile
16. A.
17. 'I'm not a carnivore, am I?' asked Saxon
18. 'Carpe diem,' said Harriet.

Unit 28C PAGE 100

1. D.
2. Language carries invaluable cultural and historical knowledge and identity, and ways of being and seeing the world.
3. These are brand names of tissues and sticky strips that cover wounds. People often use these trademarked names to refer to all brands of the products.
4. Responses will vary.
5. Responses will vary.
6. Text 1 mentions English as a living language that grows and changes. Text 2 gives examples of the ways English grows and changes over time.
7. Responses will vary.

Unit 29A PAGE 101

1. for land, religion, resources (oil, diamonds, water), politics or ideals, in the name of colonialism or racism, or pre-emptively (to strike first so you don't get struck); or over drugs or against terrorism (See lines 19–26.)
2. More effective weapons are created because of constantly improving technology. These weapons lead to more and more devastating consequences. (See lines 12–13.)
3. War damages mental health. There are no physical signs of injury but the person is wounded emotionally or psychologically and the impact of that mental health issue cannot remain hidden because there will be signs that the person is scarred on the inside.
4. Farmers cannot access their fields to grow food so whole communities suffer. Farmers risk their lives planting in their fields and lives are lost or people are maimed when landmines explode and they lose limbs. Livestock is killed by the mines.
5. the amount of money spent by governments on weapons and war as well as the amount required for rebuilding compared with the amount spent on maintaining peace or negotiating for peace
6. It takes more than one generation to rebuild after war. Generations of young people are lost during wars, especially if the wars last for years. Cities, roads and bridges are destroyed.

Unit 29B PAGE 102

1. scarred
2. insurgency
3. religion
4. international: between nations
5. Suggested answers: demolish, demolishing, demolition
6. from the Spanish *guerrilla*, which is the diminutive of *guerra* meaning war. In guerilla warfare bands of guerillas (not part of the military) use surprise attacks and sabotage to resist larger numbers of usually better-armed forces.
7. D.
8. C.
9. when one country controls or governs another country or people
10. A.
11. B.
12. which cost thousands of lives
13. might
14. probably
15. e.g. On the other hand, However
16. C.
17. The Prime Minister announced a war on drugs.
18. 'We won't commit to this war,' declared the Minister for Defence.

Unit 29C PAGE 103

1. Laureates; medal; diploma; money
2. victory/victors
3. catastrophic, groundbreaking, firestorms, obliterate
4. to engage the reader and stir an emotional response about the horrors of nuclear war
5. The theme of Text 1 is war while the main theme of Text 2 is peace. Text 2 includes specific mention of the Nobel Peace Prizes awarded in 2014 and 2017.
6. Setsuko would be very much opposed to nuclear weapons because she saw the effects firsthand of a nuclear bomb on Hiroshima.
7. Responses will vary.

Unit 30A PAGE 104

1. when there are not enough volunteers freely enlisting (See lines 2–3.)
2. by volunteering or being conscripted (See lines 2–4.)
3. C. The text generally seems neutral; however, you can infer that the writer is opposed because of the words 'forces' in paragraph 1 and 'forced' in paragraph 2; and by the way the writer pointedly includes the number of conscripts who died or were wounded. The writer also says returning soldiers were 'unfairly stigmatised' (paragraph 4).
4. Suggested answers: not having a choice; not believing in war; not agreeing with the particular war; the issue of returned soldiers being stigmatised; being a pacifist; religious or family reasons, e.g. dependent children, spouse, parents; because of a vital job or employment that could not be abandoned
5. anti-conscription: Two referendums during WWI voted against conscription. Conscription was abolished in 1959 and again in 1973. It was not popular during the Vietnam War.
6. They might not believe in a god and they might not be Australian-born. They could be recent migrants from other countries. They might have no religion or follow a religion that has no god or more than one god.

Unit 30B PAGE 105

1. soldiers
2. conscientious
3. Defence
4. reintroduced: introduced again
5. Suggested answers: volunteered, volunteering, voluntary, voluntarily
6. From the Latin *conscribere* meaning write down together (con—together; *scribere*—write down) or enrol. Conscription was first used in France in 1798 as per its current meaning: compulsory enlistment for state service, typically into the armed forces.
7. **A.**
8. **C.**
9. a medical condition of persistent mental and emotional stress caused by trauma such as war
10. **D.**
11. **B.**
12. they did not agree with
13. should
14. potentially
15. e.g. Also, Furthermore, Additionally
16. **B.**
17. 'I'd be a conscientious objector,' declared Aaron.
18. Returning Vietnam veterans did not receive a heroes' welcome in the 1970s.

Unit 30C PAGE 106

1. **D.**
2. **A.**
3. **B.**
4. The writer says that the excursion 'was really worthwhile'. They learnt a lot from the presenter; a list of some of the things learnt was also included.
5. Responses will vary. Perhaps a poster would show one of the following: happy, attractive young people smiling, working as a team, making friends, travelling and exploring the world, earning good pay, studying for a qualification, being patriotic in serving the nation, holding an Australian flag, looking smart in a uniform or proudly representing Australia.
6. Responses will vary but images portrayed would likely be death and destruction, funerals or people crying.
7. Responses will vary.

NAPLAN-style Reading Test 4 PAGES 107–108

1. **B.**
2. **B.**
3. **B**, **C** and **D.**
4. **A**, **B**, **C** and **D.**
5. he had such a pleasant, sunny face that everyone liked to buy from him
6. Text 1: **A**, **B**, **C**, **D** and **E.**
   Text 2: **A**, **B** and **C.**
7. **A.** The note at the top says 'Note: This children's book …'
8. **B.**
9. Edison invented the phonograph in 1877 'but it took a further ten years to make it a commercial success'. Also Edison took the light-bulb inventions of other inventors and worked on them, improving the inventions to make them practical and commercial. These facts tell readers that not all inventions are commercially successful.
10. **D.**
11. You can judge that it was a globally popular and impressive device because it gave him international acclaim.
12. He found the stories interesting or inspirational. He likely aspired to do great things himself from a young age. You can judge that he was ambitious.

NAPLAN-style Conventions of Language Test 4 PAGE 109

1. incandescent
2. commercially
3. prolific
4. developing
5. focused (focussed is also correct)
6. detector
7. **D.**
8. **D.**
9. **C.**
10. The incandescent light bulb
11. was
12. **C.**
13. **D.**
14. He found a book
15. **D.**
16. **B.**

ANSWERS

Updated in 2025 for the NSW Curriculum and Australian Curriculum Version 9.0 changes

ISBN 978 1 74125 652 9

Pascal Press
PO Box 250
Glebe NSW 2037
(02) 9198 1748
www.pascalpress.com.au

Publisher: Vivienne Joannou
Project editor: Mark Dixon
Edited and proofread by Mark Dixon
Answers checked by Dale Little
Cover and page design by Sonia Woo
Typeset by Grizzly Graphics (Leanne Richters)
Printed by Vivar Printing/Green Giant Press